The Principal's Hot Seat

The Principal's Hot Seat

Observing Real-World Dilemmas

Nicholas J. Pace

ROWMAN & LITTLEFIELD EDUCATION
A division of
ROWMAN & LITTLEFIELD PUBLISHERS, INC.
Lanham • New York • Toronto • Plymouth, UK

Published by Rowman & Littlefield Education
A division of Rowman & Littlefield Publishers, Inc.
A wholly owned subsidiary of The Rowman & Littlefield Publishing Group, Inc.
4501 Forbes Boulevard, Suite 200, Lanham, Maryland 20706
http://www.rowmaneducation.com

Estover Road, Plymouth PL6 7PY, United Kingdom

British Library Cataloguing in Publication Information Available

Library of Congress Cataloging-in-Publication Data

Pace, Nicholas J.
  The principal's hot seat : observing real-world dilemmas / Nicholas J. Pace.
    p. cm.
  ISBN 978-1-61048-473-2 (pbk. : alk. paper)—ISBN 978-1-61048-474-9 (electronic)
  1. High school principals—United States. 2. High schools—United States—
Administration—Decision making. 3. Leadership—United States. I. Title.
  LB2831.92.P34 2011
  373.12'011—dc23   2011036900

∞ ™ The paper used in this publication meets the minimum requirements of American National Standard for Information Sciences—Permanence of Paper for Printed Library Materials, ANSI/NISO Z39.48-1992.

Printed in the United States of America

Dedication

For the educational leadership students at the University of Northern Iowa (UNI), who have inspired me with their passion and desire to make a difference.

Contents

Acknowledgments

I am indebted to many for assistance and inspiration in this project. First and foremost, I thank the many principalship students and volunteer actors who have courageously put themselves on display in recreating the scenarios captured herein. Quite simply, the book would not exist without their creativity, generosity and courage. The students and actors are recognized individually in the section entitled "About the Contributors" at the end of the book. And of course, I'm grateful to Tom Koerner, Lynda Phung, and Kristina Mann of Rowman & Littlefield Education for their enthusiasm and assistance.

Many valued colleagues and friends at the University of Northern Iowa have also contributed mightily to this project. Several years ago, Stephen W. Taft helped me see that the role play exercise I was envisioning could be brought alive in a theater space, rather than a traditional classroom. At about the same time, Radhi H. Al-Mabuk suggested it was more than just a valuable experience for students and one about which I should write. On a gray morning at Starbuck's, John K. Smith and Deborah J. Gallagher helped me see the form and flow that the book needed. That's when it started to click.

Other faculty colleagues at UNI provided invaluable expertise related to specific cases, including Victoria P. DeFrancisco, Deborah J. Gallagher, Heather M. Olsen, Jennifer Jo Waldron, and Michael D. Waggoner. I'm also grateful for financial support provided by William P. Callahan and Dwight C. Watson, the former and present deans of the UNI College of Education respectively. Likewise, financial support from Kent M. Johnson of UNI Continuing Education and Special Programs was essential. Joe Marchensani and his staff, also recognized in the "About the Contributors" section at the end of the book, were both professional and fun, along with Keith Kennedy in the UNI Production House. My colleagues in the Friday Writer's Group, Mary Frisbee Johnson, Marybeth Stalp, and Elizabeth A. Sutton provided much-needed perspectives on the scenarios. I'm glad to be in the writing group, even though I know I've benefited more than I've contributed.

Members of the Educational Leadership and Postsecondary Education Department at UNI are both valued colleagues and trusted friends. I know many professors cannot make the same statement. Thanks to Tim Gilson, Dewitt Jones, Victoria Robinson, and Betty Hogan for their input on the project and to Marlene Shea for keeping the aforementioned away from my office door when it was closed. Graduate Assistant Emily Borcherding, also featured in the "About the Contributors" section, is an astute and efficient copy editor and all around good sport.

Finally, I thank my family for tolerating my absence and distraction while immersed in this project.

Nicholas J. Pace
Cedar Falls, IA

Preface

It's no secret that expectations for school principals are increasing. Gone are the days when a good principal was viewed as a mere manager who kept the kids in line and the building clean. Today's principals find themselves in an increasingly complex, pressure-filled environment that requires much more than was expected even a few years ago. As one urban superintendent said to me recently, "I don't need managers. I need leaders, *period.*" Despite this, most programs that prepare principals have failed to keep pace with today's needs.

In fact, Darling-Hammond, LaPointe, Meyerson, Orr, and Cohen (2007) cited a Public Agenda survey that showed a stunning 80 percent of superintendents and 69 percent of principals felt university educational leadership programs are out of touch with what happens in today's schools. While education at all levels is a frequent target for criticism, Murphy (2006) noted that the preparation of administrators is particularly shaky. Growing numbers of scholars have concluded that many educational leadership programs fail to adequately prepare principals for the myriad responsibilities they will encounter (Farkas, Johnson, & Duffett, 2003).

Levine (2005) labeled even well known programs at prestigious universities "inadequate to appalling" (p. 23). The Southern Regional Education Board (SREB) called for "departments of educational leadership to awaken from their complacency, reject the status quo and respond to appeals and criticisms from the field by identifying new content that addresses what principals need to know in order to do their jobs ..." (SREB, 2006, p. 11). Hess and Kelley (2007) concluded that programs that ignore these new realities are sending new principals into an environment for which they are simply not ready. No wonder Brock and Grady (2004, p. xi) identified "culture shock and anxiety" as normal emotions for new principals.

Enter *The Principal's Hot Seat*. As a young principal, I often found myself facing situations that were, for lack of a better term, surreal. I felt as though I was wading through scenarios that were so bizarre, emotional, or unexpected that someone was about to reveal that the whole thing was a candid camera moment or set up. But that never happened. They were *all real*. I quickly came to understand that the true life of a principal is often stranger than fiction.

In the midst of those difficult and unpredictable situations, I felt frustrated and ill-prepared to manage awkward, unexpected and intense conversations. In studying to become a principal, I'd read dozens of books and articles and written scores of papers outlining what I would do *if* . . . But I rarely had a window through which I could view the real life issues that land on the principal's desk. Beyond the unexpected complexity of the issues themselves, I was almost wholly unprepared for the way many of them would make me *feel*—full of anticipation, fear, anger, and often incredulity.

A few years later, as a professor seeking to help new principals enter this increasingly complex environment, I sought to develop an authentic experience that would provide an opportunity to improve their skills in handling these situations. Something truly authentic required more than students writing a paper about *what they thought they might do* in a particular situation.

The result was an authentic role play experience entitled *A Day in the Office*. I collaborated with professors of educational leadership and current and former principals to assemble a list of the most difficult and common dilemmas principals face. I arranged for the use of a small, wrap-around theater and made a simple mock office in which my students would assume the role of the principal.

Prior to the experience, students heard a presentation from a police officer on techniques officers use to deescalate angry people and read portions of McEwan's (2004). *How to Deal with Parents who are Angry, Troubled, Afraid, or Just Plain Crazy*. They were told to dress and carry themselves like a principal. A few students received an e-mail message from their mythical secretary the night before the exercise with some background information about their meeting, but most did not.

One by one, professors and practitioners assumed the role of the angry parent, difficult teacher, or pushy businessman and challenged my students to respond in a way that reflected the Iowa Standards for School Leaders (which mirror the ELCC standards) and their own philosophies and styles. Immediately following each scenario of approximately five minutes, students, professors, and practicing administrators debriefed the exchange, sharing observations, suggestions, and praise.

Over the past four years, we've shared some incredibly intense, memorable, and dynamic moments. Real emotion, creativity, and missteps played out live and have been captured on video. After a few days of reflection, students have described the exercise as "phenomenal" and "the most memorable and authentic learning experience I've had." The exercise, while stressful, unpredictable, and unnerving has become a highlight of the principalship program at the University of Northern Iowa.

Fifteen of the most interesting, difficult and unpredictable scenarios are contained herein. Through the use of the enclosed DVD, aspiring and practicing principals alike have the opportunity to sharpen the skills that are so vitally important but seldom effectively addressed by educational leadership programs. The fifteen real-life scenarios that have been ripped from the pages of principals' day planners are all based on reality . . . the parent who is upset about his son's suspension, the father who thinks the dynamic young teacher is far too friendly with his daughter, the coach who is convinced that a fellow teacher has a bias against athletes, and a host of other conundrums common to the principalship.

In today's complex and nuanced school environment, the principal's ability to effectively handle these issues in an appropriate, ethical, standards-based, communicative way is not just important. It is essential. *The Principal's Hot Seat* provides aspiring and practicing principals alike with the unique opportunity to observe and critique the actions of principals, while asking essential questions, such as:

- What do the standards in my state and district require me to do?
- Are the principal's actions consistent with those standards?
- What might I have done differently?
- How would I feel if a similar situation presents itself when I'm sitting in *The Principal's Hot Seat*?

USING THE SCENARIOS

Each scenario begins with a concise introduction to the issues at hand and relevant background and context. A brief overview of some relevant professional literature follows, along with a full transcript of the conversation. Following the transcript are specific questions designed to facilitate a thorough consideration of the principal's specific actions and approach in the case. After the specific questions, I invite readers to consider a number of general questions designed to explore emotions, apply standards, and consider potential twists to the case. Each scenario concludes with suggested internship or extension activities and valuable references and resources for additional reading.

The scenarios are designed to be used in a number of ways, including:

1. Homework: Students view particular scenarios on their own time and come to class prepared to share their assessment of the principal's performance.
2. In-Class Exercise: Students view particular scenarios for the first time as a group and then share and compare their assessments of the principal's performance.
3. Stop-action: While viewing a scenario for the first time, the instructor/facilitator pauses the DVD at particular points to solicit students' assessments of the principal's performance, input on what the principal should say or do next, and/or predictions for what may happen next.
4. Focus on Body Language: Try viewing the scenarios with the sound turned down to estimate the level of tension and the principal's efforts to listen, respond, and deescalate.
5. Other applications, as determined by the instructor/facilitator and students.

A FINAL COMMENT

I remind those using this book and DVD as a learning tool to remember a particularly important point: The "principals" in these scenarios are students of educational leadership who have not yet completed their program of study. Like all of us engaged in school leadership, they have much to learn. They've put their efforts to become principals on display in an extraordinarily public way, in front of their peers and professors, as well as others using this book whom they will never meet. Their efforts and generosity are worthy of respect. Rookies and veterans alike can learn from their actions.

In four years of developing, observing, and recording the scenarios and listening to the rich discussion they generate, I've learned nearly as much as the students. I've been reminded that, although we hope for decisions that are clear cut and obvious, leadership is much more complicated. I've been reminded that even with the same standards in front of us, people often come to different conclusions about what good principal leadership looks like and how to pull it off. In observing the scenarios and the discussion they generate, I've learned about interpretations I never would have expected, approaches I never would have taken, and ideas I never would have tried.

Our standards are a vital tool for effectively leading schools that strive to meet the needs of all students. At the end of the day, however, the ways in which we interact with real people to bring the standards to life are as unique as each of us. The standards may be heavy on the science of school leadership. The way leaders bring them to life is even more complicated. It's art.

Stop Picking at Kids! (High School)

Willie Barney knows his son Trevor is no angel. Thus, he was unsurprised when the call came from school: Come and pick up Trevor, who has been suspended for swearing at a teacher. Willie presents himself as a plain-spoken man who has raised his son to be respectful and do his work at school. But when he arrives in Principal Hefel-Busch's office, Willie says this is all too familiar of a story: teachers constantly pick at kids and push their buttons until they snap and get suspended, while teachers' behaviors go unchecked. It's not his son's fault.

Since the tragedy at Columbine High School, bullying has captured the attention of educators, from classrooms to research studies. Although debates about how much of this behavior is simply a part of growing up versus when it becomes harmful and dangerous are ongoing, research suggests that bullying is quite common. Card and Hodges (2008) concluded that as many as 80 percent of students have been victims at some point in school. Whether bullying comes in the school yard or cyberspace (Juvonen & Gross, 2008; Kowalski & Limber, 2007), it is usually based on ethnicity, body size, socioeconomic status, sexual orientation (Pace, 2009; Savage & Miller, 2011), or some other characteristic; we know the results can be tragic (Graham, 2010).

While peer-to-peer bullying has occupied center stage (Coloroso, 2003; Swearer, Espelage, & Napolitano, 2009), far less attention has been given to a disturbing aspect of life in schools: teachers who bully students. Acknowledging that we as educators simply enjoy some students more than others, many have taken Whitaker's (2004) advice that teachers "don't have to *like* the students; you just have to *act as if* like you like them" (italics in original) (p. 46). However, some researchers (McEvoy, 2005; Whitted & Dupper, 2008) have concluded that many teachers are unable to heed Whitaker's advice and instead engage in what McEvoy (2005) described as a "pattern of conduct, rooted in a power differential, that threatens, harms, humiliates, induces fear, or causes students substantial emotional distress" (p. 1).

While some teachers overtly mistreat students, Sylvester (2011) concluded that others bully students in more subtle, almost unnoticeable ways, such as the use of sarcasm, secret names, or arbitrary enforcement of particular policies. In many ways, privilege is invisible to those who have it or those who remain free from bullying by authority figures.

In a fascinating and extensive study of a rural Iowa high school, Carr and Kefalas (2009) examined the ways in which "teachers, parents, and other influential adults cherry-pick the young people" who seem destined for good things, offering them special treatment and frequent accolades (p. 19). "Those kids were placed on a different trajectory because the entire town was behind them, cheering for them to make it and supporting them in concrete ways" (p. 20). Students who are not seen as members of this group, argued Carr and Kefalas, received far less affirmation and investment, and often "managed to internalize the judgments from teachers" who saw limited possibilities for them (p. 65). This "authority abuse" may be nearly invisible to many, but is an important consideration for principals (McEvoy, 2005, p. 1).

In this scenario, Principal Hefel-Busch has an opportunity to hear a parent's side of the story, considering Trevor's actions and school policy. Knowing that all teachers want the support of their administrators on discipline cases, she also faces the question of whether the problem lies with Trevor, the teacher, or both.

THE TRANSCRIPT

Dad:	Well, I'm trying to figure out why my son is being suspended from school. I get a phone call saying that he cursed at a teacher. A teacher's pickin' at the kids every time I come up over here. And somebody's messin' with somebody all the time. All ya'll do is pick on people.
Principal:	Can you tell me your student's name?
Dad:	Uh, Trevor.
Principal:	Trevor, okay. Will you tell me a little bit about what happened?
Dad:	All I know is he cursed out the teacher. The teacher was pickin' at him, so he cursed at him. You tell me, you're the one that's here! You're supposed to know what's going on.
Principal:	You're right. I am. That's why I want to hear, you know, there's always more than one side to the story. So I really appreciate that you came in.

Dad:	The only side I got is a phone call saying I need to come pick him up.
Principal:	And that was today?
Dad:	That was today.
Principal:	Well, the first thing I'm really glad you came in, I appreciate you coming in to talk about it. The other thing is, is the one thing we can't have is if Trevor did curse at the teachers, that's not acceptable. We can't have that.
Dad:	Teachers shouldn't be picking at him. Every time I come up to this flippin' school that's all I hear.
Principal:	Have you met with the teacher about it?
Dad:	That's why I'm here!
Principal:	Okay. Well, that would be what I would like to do. I would kind of, since I don't know much of the story—
Dad:	What the—
Principal:	It doesn't sound like—
Dad:	Why would I want to meet with the teacher who's sitting here picking at my kids all the time?
Principal:	Well, I think it'd be a good idea to maybe solve the problem.
Dad:	What problem's going to be solved? What are you going to do differently?
Principal:	That's why I would like to meet with the teacher down here and maybe Trevor to see what we can do.
Dad:	Trevor is sitting out in the office. The teacher, like I said, every time I get a phone call . . . over and over again, ya'll continually picking at him.
Principal:	M hmm, m hmm. And I understand you feeling that way. But if Trevor is cursing at teachers or getting himself—
Dad:	Hey, I've told him not to curse at teachers. I've told him that regardless what to do. But the fact of the matter is that a bunch of adults around here that just continuously pick, pick, pick at kids! What do you expect them to do?!
Principal:	Well, I appreciate you supporting us and telling him not to curse, you know curse at teachers and get upset. I appreciate that. And I would really like us to work it out. Because if someone is picking on Trevor. Ya know. If it is because people are human . . . and if there is that relationship isn't there between you and the teacher then I would like to get that worked out.
Dad:	You guys don't have relationships with anybody!
Principal:	Oh, yeah, I think we do. I think we do. I mean I'm really glad you came in. You know. That's a start. I'm glad you support us at home and tell Trevor not to, you know, that he shouldn't engage in those, you know, name calling or disrespect towards the adults. I mean, we appreciate that.

Dad:	But he's a kid. Kids are going to do those things. If the adult does it, the kid's gonna do it.
Principal:	You're right.
Dad:	So what do you do with a teacher who's picking at kids?
Principal:	Well, that would be my responsibility.
Dad:	And that's what I'm asking you. What do you do with kids? You're kicking him out of school. I know what's happening to my son. What's gonna happen to a teacher who is continuously picking at kids?
Principal:	Well the first thing I'm going to do is I'm going to meet with the teacher and I'm gonna try to find out what's happening. How things are going. I would like to talk to Trevor. We can do that together or we can do that, ya know, at a different time.
Dad:	And then what?
Principal:	Then we're going to get back together and we're going to come up with a plan.
Dad:	So how does that fix the teacher's behavior that is continuously picking at my son?
Principal:	Well hopefully it's not going to continuously happen. We're going to figure out what's going on and we're going to fix it.
Dad:	So what is the consequence for the teacher?
Principal:	Right now, I'm going to meet with the teacher. And hopefully figure out what's going on. I want to meet with Trevor.
Dad:	So if you figure out the teacher's picking at my kid, what are you gonna do?
Principal:	Well, if there is the relationship, if there is a problem with the relationship, my suggestion at that point is there are a few things we can do. We maybe move Trevor into a different classroom . . . maybe have a different teacher.
Dad:	That's what I want. I want him moved to a different classroom because I'm tired of him picking on him. The fact of the matter is I don't know what difference it will make, because all of your teachers pick at people anyways.
Principal:	Well, I would like for us to meet with Trevor and the teacher first before we make that decision. You know. Would you be willing to do that?
Dad:	I've already talked to him; he's a fool!
Principal:	The teacher?
Dad:	Yes! And if he gets loud with me I'm gonna whoop his butt across the street! I'm tired of dealing with him!
Principal:	Right, Right. And I understand that. We don't want that to happen. You know, this is what I would like to do. You know. If you don't want to meet with the teacher, then I'll meet with the teacher and

then the two of us and Trevor can get back together and go from there. But if the relationship is this bad, if the bridge is burned this badly, then maybe it is in the best interest for Trevor to be moved to a different class.

Dad: Alright. That's what I want. I want him moved.

Principal: Okay, so how about today you take Trevor home. Um, he's probably pretty upset, I can tell you are pretty upset. Again, I appreciate you coming in to talk to me. And then I'll do some talking with the teacher and maybe a couple of the other teachers too and see maybe where we can best put Trevor . . . for a different, for a different teacher.

Dad: Thank you.

Principal: You're welcome.

DISCUSSION AND REFLECTION QUESTIONS

1. Identify the key issue(s).
2. Identify the secondary issue(s).
3. After thanking Dad for coming in, the principal explains (at 0:50) that Trevor using profanity toward the teacher is unacceptable. Dad responds by complaining that the teacher "shouldn't be picking at him." Given that many teachers identify issues related to respect as frequent reasons for office referrals, how should she respond? Is it possible that there is a cultural or generational issue between the teacher and students? Is it possible that Dad is simply deflecting blame for the situation toward the teacher?
4. At 1:41 Dad explains that he has told Trevor not to curse at teachers but goes on to say, "Fact of the matter is that the adults around here that just continuously pick, pick, pick at kids! What do you expect them to do?!" How should she respond to the question? Have you known teachers who "push students' buttons?"
5. Principal Hefel-Busch discusses the importance of relationships. Dad counters that if kids see teachers drawing kids into verbal exchanges like this, kids will respond negatively, to which the principal agrees. Dad then asks (at 2:46) what she's going to do with "a teacher who is continuously picking at kids." How should the principal respond?
6. At 3:07 Dad is still pressing to know what the principal will do with the teacher's behavior. In saying that, "Hopefully it's not going to continuously happen. We're going to figure out what's going on and we're going to fix it," is Principal Hefel-Busch implying that she believes the teacher *is* picking at Trevor?

7. Dad continues to demand to know what will be done with the teacher if the principal determines that he is, in fact, picking at students. The principal floats the possibility of moving Trevor to another teacher's classroom. Is this a good idea? Does it effectively address the issue?

8. At 3:40 Dad jumps on the idea of moving Trevor to a different classroom, but also complains that it may not do any good "because all of your teachers pick at people anyways." Is that a sign of an impossible parent or a more pervasive problem among the faculty? How can she know?

9. Principal Hefel-Busch suggests a meeting to discuss the issue. Dad complains that he has already talked to him and "he's a fool." He goes on to say, (3:59) "If he gets loud with me I'm gonna whoop his butt across the street! I'm tired of dealing with him!" How should the principal respond? Do you interpret this as frustration or a threat?

10. At 4:19 the principal suggests that if the relationship between Trevor and the teacher is badly damaged, that perhaps Trevor should be moved to a different class. Is this an appropriate course of action or should she proceed with the meeting with Trevor and the teacher? Could moving Trevor trigger a rash of other parents wanting their children moved?

11. Identify areas in which you believe the principal acted effectively.

12. Identify areas in which you believe the principal could have acted more effectively.

Balcony View

Generally speaking, how did the principal perform in this scenario? What would you have done differently?

Standards In Action

Which standards do you see as relevant in the scenario? Does the principal effectively meet them? Are there standards and/or criteria left unmet by the principal's actions?

Self Check

Picturing yourself in the principal's chair, describe your emotions. Does the case touch any of your biases or prior experiences?

Switch It Up

How might your thinking or approach change if the gender, social class, ethnicity, language, age, sexual orientation or other descriptors of the players involved were different?

Principal's Presence

In televised presidential debates, "looking presidential" is an important measure of a candidate's performance. The same is true for principals. Halpern and Lubar (2003, p. 3) define leadership presence as being more than "commanding attention" to include "the ability to connect authentically with the thoughts and feelings of others." Does the principal exert an effective "Principal's Presence?" Explain.

Principal's Priority

How *serious* is the situation?
How *soon* should the principal address this situation?
Should the principal inform/involve a *supervisor* on this issue?

In A Word

Capture the principal's performance in the scenario using one word.

Collaborate

Collaborate with a classmate or colleague to rewrite or alter the case with a different set of circumstances. Share your new case with other colleagues to ascertain how they would approach it.

Extension & Internship Experiences

- Does your building have data on specific reasons for office referrals? If so, identify the top reasons. Are there commonly defined and practiced definitions of concepts like "respect" or "insubordination?" Can the data be disaggregated by teacher, classroom, student demographics, etc.? What conclusions could be drawn?
- Does your building/district conduct surveys with stakeholders to ascertain their perception of issues like those raised by Dad? If so, how is the data used? If not, should such a survey be constructed and administered?

- Are there some teachers who frequently have difficulty interacting with particular groups of students (related to gender, ethnicity, language, social class, sexual orientation, etc.)? Has your building or district engaged in professional development related to cultural competency?

REFERENCES AND RESOURCES

Card, N. A., & Hodges, E. V. E. (2008). Peer victimization among schoolchildren: Correlations, causes, consequences, and considerations in assessment and intervention. *School Psychology Quarterly, 23*(4), 451–461.

Carr, P. J., & Kefalas, M. J. (2009). *Hollowing out the middle: The rural brain drain and what it means for America.* Boston, MA: Beacon Press.

Coloroso, B. (2003). *The bully, the bullied, and the bystander.* New York, NY: HarperCollins.

Graham, S. (2010). What educators need to know about bullying behaviors. *Phi Delta Kappan, 92*(1), 66–69. Retrieved from EBSCO*host*.

Juvonen, J., & Gross, E. F. (2008). Extending the school grounds? Bullying experiences in cyberspace. *Journal of School Health, 78*(9), 496–505.

Kowalski, R. M., & Limber, S. P. (2007). Electronic bullying among middle school students. *Journal of Adolescent Health, 41*(6), S22–S30.

McEvoy, A. (2005). Teachers who bully students: Patterns and policy implications. Paper presented at the Hamilton Fish Institute's Persistently Safe Schools Conference, Philadelphia, PA. Retrieved from http://www.stopbullyingnow.com/teachers%20who%20bully%20 students%20McEvoy.pdf

Olweus, D. (1993). *Bullying at school: What we know and what we can do.* Oxford, UK: Blackwell Publishers.

Pace, N. J. (2009). *The principal's challenge: Learning from gay and lesbian students.* Charlotte, NC: Information Age.

Raffaele-Mendez, L. M., & Knoff, H. M. (2003). Who gets suspended from school and why: A demographic analysis of schools and disciplinary infractions in a large school. *Education and Treatment of Children, 26*(1), 30–s51.

Reschney, S. M. (2008). *Teachers who bully students: The parents' perspectives.* (Unpublished master's thesis). University of Saskatchewan, Saskatchewan. Retrieved from http://sundog.usask.ca/record=b2888574~S8

Rodríguez, L. F. (2005). Yo, mister! An alternative urban high school offers lessons on respect. *Educational Leadership, 62*(7), 78–80.

Savage, D., & Miller, T. (Eds.) (2011). *It gets better: Coming out, overcoming bullying, and creating a life worth living.* New York, NY: Dutton Adult.

Swearer, S. M., Espelage, D. L., & Napolitano, S. A. (2009). *Bullying prevention and intervention: Realistic strategies for schools.* New York, NY: The Guilford Press.

Sylvester, R. (2011). Teacher as bully: Knowingly or unintentionally harming students. *The Delta Kappa Gamma Bulletin, 77*(2), 42–45.

Teel, K. M., & Obidah, J. E. (2008). *Building racial and cultural competence in the classroom: Strategies from urban educators.* New York, NY: Teachers College Press.

Twenlow, S. W., Fonagy, P., Sacco, F. C., & Brethour, Jr., J. R. (2006). Teachers who bully students: A hidden trauma. *International Journal of Social Psychiatry, 52*(3), 187–198.

Whitaker, T. (2004). *What great teachers do differently: Fourteen things that matter most.* Larchmont NY: Eye on Education.

Whitted, K. S., & Dupper, D. R. (2008). Do teachers bully students? Findings from a survey of students in an alternative education setting. *Education and Urban Society, 40*(3), 329-341.

I Get Him Here, You Send Him Home (Middle School)

Every educator is familiar with the old adage: The parents teachers really need to see usually don't attend conferences. Mr. Coulter is that kind of parent and today is a rare and unexpected opportunity for Principal Boyd to have a much-needed conversation about young John Coulter's attendance and school performance.

On this unplanned visit, the frustrated Mr. Coulter acknowledges his son's problems and how he struggles to get him to school. He says the school's attendance policy has his son locked in a senseless cycle of absence and suspension. If and when he gets John to school, he's suspended for excessive absences, while his grades and motivation decline further. And so it goes.

The social, educational, and financial costs of truancy are high, including poor school performance and dropping out (Alsbaugh, 1998; Henry & Hunzinga, 2007) and substance abuse (Bell, Rosen, & Dynlacht, 1994; Bryant & Zimmerman, 2002). Other research has linked truancy to higher rates of risky sexual behaviors and teen pregnancy (Leitenberg & Saltzman, 2000) and increased danger of auto accidents (McCartt, Shabanova, & Leaf, 2003). While schools have no magic wands at their disposal, school and community partnerships that focus on holistic causes of truancy have shown promise (Huck, 2010; Murphy & Tobin, 2010; Rodriguez & Conchas, 2009).

As the scenario unfolds, Mr. Coulter paints a familiar picture. His son, a student with multiple needs, seems to be falling through the cracks of policy, in spite of adults' best efforts. Since current practice is clearly not working, Principal Boyd finds herself trying to explain a seemingly ineffective school policy to a disgruntled and surly father, dispense parenting advice without offending, while at the same time trying to come up with a workable solution.

THE TRANSCRIPT

Dad: . . .Why, if my son won't come to school, when he does come to school you turn around and put him right back out . . . tell me how that makes sense. You want him there. When he gets there you send him home. Why?

Principal: Okay, I totally understand your concern. What is your son's name?

Visitor: You do?

Principal: From what I hear, yes I do. What is your son's name, sir?

Dad: John.

Principal: John, okay, yep, I'm familiar with John. From what I can, um, remember about the situation, and actually I know you son. He's very pleasant . . . a couple of concerns that we talked about . . . Some of the concerns, we have a couple of policies in place. Um . . .

Dad: I don't care what your policy says. He's not coming to school. When he comes to school you send him home. Explain! It doesn't make sense.

Principal: And you know what, sir, I understand your concerns. And as a parent myself, that would be frustrating for me. But in school we have rules that are required. We have behavioral policies, we have attendance policies, and those are all rules that we have to follow. And, um, if you have a specific concern, our concern could be a number of things. And again, I totally understand your frustration.

Dad: But I can't get him out of bed, and when I get him out of bed, because he's missed so much school and I finally get his little lazy butt to school, and then you turn around a half hour later and call me and tell me he's suspended because he's skipped school.

Principal: Okay

Dad: I don't care what your policy says it doesn't make sense, because that's what's happened. I'm trying to get him out of bed. I get him out of bed, I get him there and you send him back home.

Principal: If skipping school is the issue, and clearly in this situation it is, we have policies that state you need to be in school a certain number of days, a certain number of times. Unless he has an excuse from you, an excuse that says . . .

Dad: He's lazy! He doesn't have an excuse!

Principal: Okay. And in that case we may need to look at some other options. We have a home school worker here in our building that would be more than happy to accommodate you if . . .

Dad:	She's been over there. She can't get him out of bed either.
Principal:	Okay. And so then we may need to explore some more options together.
Dad:	We even called one time to get a ride and nobody would come to get him.
Principal:	Our home school worker's job is to be, kind of a liaison between the school and yourself, and we'd be more than happy to accommodate you.
Dad:	Can she pick him up every morning?
Principal:	If that's the need, then yes we would be more than happy, we want John at school. We need him here. He has to be here in order to be successful. We want him here. And I also want it to be a partnership between myself, the school, and you. It doesn't only need to be your responsibility, or only my responsibility. We need to be able to work together.
Dad:	Then why are you sending him back home?
Principal:	What we need to do . . .
Dad:	He's flunking. He's gonna do eighth grade again.
Principal:	And I understand that. We have a couple of programs that may interest and accommodate his need. We have the Echoes program. We have extended day program. We have, um, some teachers that are willing to give up their lunch time to work with your student. We have all of these things.
Dad:	If he won't come to school during a regular school day, what makes you think that he's going to stay after school and then he's not going to come back after school when you sent him home for skipping?
Principal:	Okay. And I understand that sir. You have some very valid concerns. I just want to talk about how we can work together to get your son here.
Dad:	It's not working.
Principal:	That much is true. I agree. I agree. If the issue is getting up, not being able to get up in the morning, maybe we should consider what time he's going to bed, some of the activities he's a part of.
Dad:	All the boy does is sleep.
Principal:	Okay. Well then you know what, maybe we can have our school psychologist just have a conversation with him.
Dad:	Can she come to the house? Because I can't get him to school, and when I get him to school you turn him right back around.
Principal:	Okay and if that's the . . .
Dad:	She make home visits?
Principal:	Yes, we all make home visits. We all are more than happy to . . . whatever you need done, sir. Again, we want John at school. It's

important for him to be in school. He has to be in school to be successful. So whatever it takes, whatever we need to do, I'm more than happy to do that. What I want to do is sit down with the team, the school psychologist, the home school worker, and our school counselor . . .

Dad: That sounds great, but you're going to have to come get him.

Principal: Okay.

Dad: You're going to have to bring the whole crew to the house.

Principal: And you know what, again, whatever we need to do. We can make that happen. I'll be more than happy to do that.

Dad: What about the teachers who won't give him any homework?

Principal: What I want to do is meet with that team first and then I think the second step . . .

Dad: It's out of sight, out of mind. If he's not there, they don't mind if he's not there. And when he gets to school, which is a struggle, you turn around and send him home.

Principal: And I apologize that you feel that way . . .

Dad: I try. I burn up their phone lines, I fill up their email boxes. I get nothing.

Principal: Let me have that conversation with my first team. And then I will talk to my teachers. Because if that is happening, that is a valid concern and that needs to be addressed. So, let me speak with the first team and then my team of teachers and then let's say three days from now, Wednesday about 3:00 o'clock I can give you a call and update you on the situation.

Dad: Do I gotta bring him with me?

Principal: Actually, you know what, we can have a phone conversation first and then at that time we'll talk about the best time to meet.

Dad: He needs to be here. I wanna bring him in.

Principal: Okay, yep. That sounds good. Okay.

Dad: If I can find him. If you haven't put him out of school yet, again.

Principal: Sir, I understand your concern. I do. And you know what? I just want to thank you for coming to see me. I appreciate you not just kind of letting it go and you wanting to address the situation.

Dad: I got that letter from that stinking computer and that phone system keeps calling me wanting to know where my kid's at.

Principal: Yeah, It's a pretty nice system.

Dad: No. It's getting old.

Principal: Okay. And I understand again sir. I really understand your concerns. But I really, really wanna, um address the issue. I want to get it taken care of . . ..

DISCUSSION AND REFLECTION QUESTIONS

1. Identify the key issue(s).
2. Identify the secondary issue(s).
3. At 7:12 Dad asks if the home school worker will pick John up for school every morning. Does Principal Boyd over-promise in her response? Can she make this commitment? If your school has an employee of this type, what are the person's responsibilities? If not, who most often deals with these issues? Would picking John up for school, perhaps even waking him up, remove too much of the family's responsibility? On the other hand, Dad and Principal Boyd seem to agree that things are not working as they are now.
4. At 7:25 she speaks of a partnership and shared responsibility for John's success in school. Dad responds by asking why the school consistently sends him back home. In your opinion, is Dad seeking help, venting, looking for a fight, making excuses, or something else? What should Principal Boyd say to Dad's pointed question?
5. At 7:40 the principal identifies a number of school programs designed to help struggling students like John. Again, Dad responds by asking, "What makes you think that he's going to stay after school and then he's not going to come back after school when you sent him home for skipping?" How should she respond?
6. At 9:25 Dad complains that he gets no response from messages he leaves with teachers. How should she respond?
7. At 9:50 Principal Boyd and Dad are discussing next steps. The principal suggests that it is not necessary to have John at the next meeting. Dad disagrees and says he wants to bring John, and the principal quickly switches positions and agrees. Is this a good decision or is she allowing Dad too much control over the situation?
8. Identify areas in which you believe the principal acted effectively.
9. Identify areas in which you believe the principal could have acted more effectively.

Balcony View

Generally speaking, how did the principal perform in this scenario? What would you have done differently?

Standards In Action

Which standards do you see as relevant in the scenario? Does the principal effectively meet them? Are there standards and/or criteria left unmet by the principal's actions?

Self Check

Picturing yourself in the principal's chair, describe your emotions. Does the case touch any of your biases or prior experiences?

Switch It Up

How might your thinking or approach change if the gender, social class, ethnicity, language, age, sexual orientation or other descriptors of the players involved were different?

Principal's Presence

In televised presidential debates, "looking presidential" is an important measure of a candidate's performance. The same is true for principals. Halpern and Lubar (2003, p. 3) define leadership presence as being more than "commanding attention" to include "the ability to connect authentically with the thoughts and feelings of others." Does the principal exert an effective "Principal's Presence?" Explain.

Principal's Priority

How *serious* is the situation?
How *soon* should the principal address this situation?
Should the principal inform/involve a *supervisor* on this issue?

In A Word

Capture the principal's performance in the scenario using one word.

Collaborate

Collaborate with a classmate or colleague to rewrite or alter the case with a different set of circumstances. Share your new case with other colleagues to ascertain how they would approach it.

Extension & Internship Experiences

- Interview the building or district official responsible for school attendance, truancy, and parent liaison duties. What policies or programs are in place?
- Ask a mentor to describe efforts he or she has seen succeed in addressing problems like this.

• Examine your building's suspension and attendance data. What trends emerge? What action, if any, is being taken related to the trends?

REFERENCES AND RESOURCES

Alspaugh, J. W. (1998). Maybe schools encourage dropping out. *American Secondary Education, 25,* 10–11.

Bell, A. J., Rosen, L. A., & Dynlacht, D. (1994). Truancy intervention. *Journal of Research and Development in Education, 27,* 203–211.

Bryant, A. L., & Zimmerman, M. A. (2002). Examining the effects of academic beliefs and behaviors on changes in substance use among urban adolescents. *Journal of Educational Psychology, 94,* 621–637.

Bye, L., Alvarez, M. E., Haynes, J., & Sweigart, C. E. (2010). *Truancy prevention and intervention: A practical guide.* New York, NY: Oxford University Press.

Franklin, C., Harris, M. B., & Allen-Mears, P. (Eds.). (2008). *The school practitioner's concise companion to preventing dropout and attendance problems.* New York, NY: Oxford University Press.

Henry, K. L., & Huizinga, D. H. (2007a). School-related risk and protective factors associated with truancy among urban youth placed at risk. *The Journal of Primary Prevention, 28,* 505–519.

Huck, J. L. (2010, October 31). Truancy programs: Are the effects too easily washed away? *Education and Urban Society.* doi: 10.1177/001312451038071

Kearney, C. A. (2008). *Helping school refusing students and their parents: A guide for school-based professionals.* New York, NY: Oxford University Press.

Lamdin, D. J. (1996). Evidence of student attendance as an independent variable in education production functions. *Journal of Educational Research, 89,* 155–162.

Leitenberg, H., & Saltzman, H. (2000). A statewide survey of age at first intercourse for adolescent females and age of their male partners: Relation to other risk behaviors and statutory rape implications. *Archives of Sexual Behavior, 29,* 203–215.

McCartt, A. T., Shabanova, V. I., & Leaf, W. A. (2003). Driving experience, crashes and traffic citations of teenage beginning drivers. *Accident Analysis and Prevention, 35,* 311–320.

Morris, R. C., & Howard, A. C. (2003). Designing an effective in-school suspension program. *Clearing House, 76*(3), 156–159.

Murphy, J., & Tobin, K. (2010). *Homelessness comes to school.* Thousand Oaks, CA: Corwin Press.

Rodriguez, L. F., & Conchas, G. Q. (2009). Preventing truancy and dropout among urban middle school youth: Understanding community-based action from the student's perspective. *Education and Urban Society, 41*(2), 216–247.

Hot Seat #3

I'm Afraid of Him, Afraid for My Job (High School)

Some principals thrive on the unpredictability of the job. Others say that unpredictability is precisely what makes it so stressful. Either way, one never knows what crisis may come through the door next. Marybeth, a hard-working teacher aide, proves it when she comes to Principal Tullis' office.

Marybeth explains that she and Jim, a math teacher, were involved in a romantic relationship before she broke it off few months ago. In Principal Tullis' office, she reveals that Jim has been pressuring her to resume their relationship. She's finding it increasingly awkward to work effectively on district-required committees with Jim. To further complicate matters, Jim also serves on the budget committee, which is charged with identifying cost saving measures as budget cuts loom. Marybeth worries Jim may use his influence on the budget committee to eliminate her job if she doesn't resume the relationship. She's afraid and looking for help.

Teacher aides and associates play a vital role in schools. From clerical duties like making copies to extra one-to-one assistance with students, they provide stretched teachers with essential help. When the teacher and associate have an effective working relationship, students can benefit greatly. Giangreco, Suter, and Doyle (2010) noted that on a given day we might expect to see teacher aides or paraprofessionals present in almost any classroom in the United States. In fact, the researchers cited a 2005 U.S. Department of Education report noting that nearly 400,000 special education teacher aides were employed nationally and that nearly 40 percent of school districts employed more special education paraprofessionals than special education teachers. Despite the growing and important role teacher aides play in schools, Riggs and Mueller (2001) noted aides are often poorly trained, unclear about their responsibilities, and frustrated by procedures and lack of support. The researchers noted that "perhaps the most striking aspect of the research was the paraeducators' acknowledgment of the complex and intense relationships that developed between various members of the school community . . ." (p. 59).

In this case, the intensity yielded a romantic relationship that, according to Marybeth, now constitutes potential harassment. Fortunately, schools have clearly articulated policies prohibiting sexual harassment, along with procedures for reporting complaints, though Marybeth seems unclear about what to do. Dunklee and Shoop (2006) noted that schools are "liable for environmental harassment if senior management does not take immediate and appropriate steps to terminate harassing conduct and discipline the offending party" (p. 314). At the same time, Dunklee and Shoop (2006) asserted that false accusations of harassment can devastate an educator's reputation and destroy a career. For this reason, "if an action is proved to be true, then definitive action to punish must be demonstrated. If the action is proved false, then definitive action should be taken to punish the false accuser" (p. 324).

Brock and Grady (2004, p. 49) observed that "school leadership sometimes involves listening to the personal problems of staff members" and that the principal is often "viewed as a sympathetic listener or a trusted source of guidance." Brock and Grady also advised that staff members often need to discuss these issues, but cautioned principals from getting too involved and taking "ownership of staff members' personal problems" (p. 49). Many problems should be addressed by trained professionals.

Principal Tullis' office is the first stop on the complicated path toward understanding just what has happened between Jim and Marybeth, what should happen next and how involved he should become.

THE TRANSCRIPT

Principal:	Hi Mary Beth, how are you?
Teacher Aide:	Hi. Thanks for meeting with me. I really appreciate it.
Principal:	Oh, no problem. Let's sit down here together.
Teacher Aide:	I need to talk to you about something and I would like this to remain confidential if possible.
Principal:	Absolutely, okay.
Teacher Aide:	Um, so I've been here just for a short while as you know. And I really like my job. I really like the school. And I've got some things going on that I need to talk to you about. But overall I really just want to emphasize that I really love this job and really want to keep this job. And I know with the funding decisions and all that kind of stuff, I just, I don't want to be

on the radar, in any way problematic. And I know that the decisions are made by lots and lots of people. But I have some concerns about one of the people in charge of making the decisions. Um, Jim, right. So, Jim is, is one of our colleagues, and we have to work together an awful lot. And I'm not sure if you're aware of this, but we did have some personal relationship issues that . . . I guess that's what I need to talk to you about because it's really becoming problematic. And I'm not really sure who to talk to about it. But I'm really worried about my job, so . . . um, I'm really a very professional person. And Jim approached me very professionally. And we had common interests, and we hung out, and we just were very public about our relationship and were very professional and tried to keep everything above board because that's how I work. But I found that we had things that weren't in common, and I broke it off with him, and he just hasn't taken it very well. And so what's been happening is he's really taken it upon himself to be quite cleverly bothering me in what I would call problematic ways. So he's been pressuring me a lot to continue the relationship and I don't want to. But I really think that he would throw out the getting rid of me card as soon as he could. And so I really . . .

Principal: Can I stop you for just a second? I mean, ultimately what do you want? . . . and I see you're upset. And, and ya know I just want you to know that anytime you need somebody to listen to or work with this that I'll be here to help you . . . But ultimately I mean what do you want? At the very end, how do you see this being handled?

Teacher Aide: Well, I just want it to stop! And I don't want anybody to know about it. Because I'm just embarrassed now . . . and I feel terribly about it . . . and I just want it to stop . . . but you just can't tell him. I mean, I just . . . I can't have him know that he's had this much control over me. And I just . . . It's just gotten beyond. And I can't . . . I just don't even know what to do. But you just can't tell anybody. You just can't! It's just something . . .

Principal: Well what do you suggest? What do you want me to do?

Teacher Aide: I don't know. That's why I came to you. Because I don't know what to do actually . . .

Principal: I don't know either . . .

Teacher Aide: And I have no idea and I just can't lose my job. I mean I just love this job. And it's just such an important part of me, and I just . . . I just don't even know what to do! And I . . .

Principal: Well let's stop for just a minute and take a few deep breaths. And it's going to be okay. I want you to know that . . . that I do want to do whatever it takes to help you . . . and we're going to work on this together. So just breathe in, breathe out.

Teacher Aide: But we have to work together. I mean it's required by the district that we have to be on all this interdisciplinary collaboration. And I support it wholeheartedly, but not with him. And so I just I don't know how to be professional because he's not being professional. And here's what he's doing . . . he's being, like off-camera, he's being off sight, and he's bothering me at home. And to report anything would involve, you know, like restraining orders and things like that and I just don't want to do any of that kind of stuff.

Principal: I really think that I need some time to think about this. I have a lot of this to absorb. But I'm confident that there's a way we can get through this. Okay? And there's a way we can retain your dignity and get what's best for everybody. Okay?

Teacher Aide: But I haven't done anything wrong.

Principal: Oh, absolutely not.

Teacher Aide: I haven't done anything wrong, and I know what he's going to do because this is just how it works in life . . . and women always get the short shrift . . . I mean, it's terrible!

Principal: I've seen your work and I think that you are great at what you do. And you know what else? I was gonna ask you, have you ever thought about becoming a teacher, a professional educator? I mean what kind of schooling do you have? What would it take?

Teacher Aide: Well, I can think about that, but I don't know what that has to do with what we're talking about.

Principal: Well, it would be a way to get your mind off things, number one, and become busy with something else, and ultimately it could be a way that, you know, you could distance yourself from him.

Teacher Aide: So what about the working together stuff? I mean, is there any way to just get me off the committee?

Principal: That's a really hard one. I really need to think about that.

Teacher Aide: I just . . . I can't . . . I really can't take it!

Principal: I'm pretty good about being creative and I think that there's a way that we can make it so that nobody will know.

Teacher Aide: Okay. And you won't tell anybody?

Principal: Oh, absolutely not. I give you my word that I'm not gonna go out and blab it.

Teacher Aide: Okay . . . Thanks.

Principal: You're welcome.

Teacher Aide: Okay. I'm going to need a couple of minutes to just . . .

DISCUSSION AND REFLECTION QUESTIONS

1. Identify the key issue(s).
2. Identify the secondary issue(s).
3. At 12:36 Principal Tullis asks if he can stop Marybeth and asks "ultimately, what do you want?" Is this an effective way to find out what Marybeth is seeking from him? Or is the question premature because he has not heard enough of the story? Explain.
4. At 12:44 Principal Tullis tells Marybeth that he will be available anytime she needs someone to listen to her. Is he inserting himself into a relationship issue in which he should not be involved or demonstrating that he wants to help Marybeth? Explain.
5. At 14:01 Marybeth says, "Here's what he's doing . . . " and proceeds to describe Jim's actions. Evaluate the principal's response. Should he let her talk, press for more information, or respond as he does? Why?
6. At 14:45 Principal Tullis asks Marybeth if she has ever thought about becoming a professional teacher. She responds by saying it is something she could think about but that she is not sure what that has to do with the current issue. Principal Tullis responds by saying, "It would be a way to get your mind off things, number one, become busy with something else and ultimately it could be a way that you could distance yourself from him."

   Is this a good approach? Do you think Principal Tullis is merely trying to help her get her mind on something else and not address the alleged harassment in a meaningful way? Does the idea of getting her mind off things and distancing Marybeth from Jim imply that the principal is not taking her concerns seriously?

   On the other hand, is Principal Tullis providing Marybeth with some expert mentoring and affirmation by suggesting that her skills are underutilized as a teacher's associate? Is he opening a door of opportunity that will help her move from a teacher associate's role to that of a teacher?
7. At 15:11 Marybeth presses Principal Tullis for an answer about the requirement that she participate on district-required initiatives with Jim. She asks if she can be removed from the committee. Given her level of concern, how should he respond? Would removing her from the committee be an option, in your opinion? Would doing so effectively address the issues at hand?
8. At 15:28 Principal Tullis assures Marybeth that he won't tell anyone about the issues she has raised. Is this a good idea? Why or why not? Is he ethically bound to maintain confidentiality or to investigate what she has shared? Are there situations in which principals might be asked to maintain confidence, but cannot do so?
9. Identify areas in which you believe the principal acted effectively.

10. Identify areas in which you believe the principal could have acted more effectively.

Balcony View

Generally speaking, how did the principal perform in this scenario? What would you have done differently?

Standards In Action

Which standards do you see as relevant in the scenario? Does the principal effectively meet them? Are there standards and/or criteria left unmet by the principal's actions?

Self Check

Picturing yourself in the principal's chair, describe your emotions. Does the case touch any of your biases or prior experiences?

Switch It Up

How might your thinking or approach change if the gender, social class, ethnicity, language, age, sexual orientation or other descriptors of the players involved were different?

Principal's Presence

In televised presidential debates, "looking presidential" is an important measure of a candidate's performance. The same is true for principals. Halpern and Lubar (2003, p. 3) define leadership presence as being more than "commanding attention" to include "the ability to connect authentically with the thoughts and feelings of others." Does the principal exert an effective "Principal's Presence?" Explain.

Principal's Priority

How *serious* is the situation?
How *soon* should the principal address this situation?
Should the principal inform/involve a *supervisor* on this issue?

In A Word

Capture the principal's performance in the scenario using one word.

Collaborate

Collaborate with a classmate or colleague to rewrite or alter the case with a different set of circumstances. Share your new case with other colleagues to ascertain how they would approach it.

Extension & Internship Experiences

- Does your building or district have a policy on relationship issues between staff members?
- To whom are employees supposed to report harassment in the workplace? Interview the official charged with responding to issues of this type. Review the steps taken and forms used.
- Does your building/district offer professional development related to issues centered on harassment?

REFERENCES AND RESOURCES

Alexander, K., & Alexander, D. M. (2012). *American public school law.* (8th ed.). Belmont, CA: Wadsworth.

Brock, B. L., & Grady, M. L. (2004). *Launching your first principalship: A guide for beginning principals.* Thousand Oaks, CA: Corwin Press.

Conn, C. (2004). *Bullying and harassment: A legal guide for educators.* Alexandria, VA: Association for Curriculum Development.

Dunklee, D. R., & Shoop, R. J. (2006). *The principal's quick-reference guide to school law: Reducing liability, litigation and other potential legal tangles.* Thousand Oaks, CA: Corwin Press.

Giangreco, M. F., Suter, J. C., & Doyle, M. (2010). Paraprofessionals in Inclusive Schools: A Review of Recent Research. *Journal of Educational & Psychological Consultation, 20*(1), 41–57. doi: 10.1080/10474410903535356

Howard, L. G. (2007). *The sexual harassment handbook: Everything you need to know before someone calls a lawyer.* Franklin Lakes, NJ: The Career Press.

Meritor Savings Bank v. Vinson, 477 U.S. 57 (1986).

Meyer, E. J. (2008). Gendered harassment in secondary schools: Understanding teachers' (non) interventions. *Gender & Education, 20*(6), 555–570. doi: 10.1080/09540250802213115

Riggs, C. G., & Mueller, P. H. (2001). Employment and utilization of paraeducators in inclusive settings. *Journal of Special Education, 35*(1), 54–62.

Who Called DHS?
(Elementary School)

Mr. Jon Cox, an African American father of an elementary boy, extends a pleasant greeting to Principal Deb Donlea when he arrives at her office unannounced. The pleasantries fade quickly, however, as he demands to know who placed a call to the state Department of Human Services (DHS) about a possible case of child abuse involving his son. As Mr. Cox demands to know who made the call, he unleashes a barrage of profanity. In the midst of Mr. Cox's anger, Principal Donlea faces difficult questions involving culture, parenting techniques, and the school's role in protecting children.

Perhaps no professional responsibility is greater than an educator's role as a mandatory reporter of possible child abuse. However, specific policies and procedures, such as which school officials are made aware of reports differ across schools. Further, Dunklee and Shoop (2006, p. 292) noted legal differences in states requiring educators to report cases in which they have "reason to believe" or "reason to suspect" abuse. Though these definitions can be slippery, best practice is to focus on what a reasonable person in a similar situation would likely conclude. Commonly cited signs of neglect or abuse may include sadness, hostility, frequent fighting, and reluctance to go home. While these signs have been *associated* with abuse, they cannot be viewed as *indicators* or absolute evidence. Rather, they are *cues* that should trigger the application of common sense and school policy.

Parental use of corporal punishment has generated a great deal of debate, research, and controversy. Grogan-Kaylor and Otis (2007) noted that most parents have, at some time, spanked their children. Others have found that parents in rural areas and the Southern United States are more likely to employ corporal punishment and that boys are more frequently spanked than girls (Giles-Sims, Straus & Sugarman, 1995). Though some associate spanking with lower socioeconomic status families, Grogan-Kaylor and Otis (2007) pointed out that the connection between socioeconomic status and corporal punishment has been inconsistent. McLoyd and Smith (2002) and Grogan-Kaylor and Otis (2007) have found that, in comparison to white families, African American families are more likely to use corporal punishment.

Others have examined the way schools communicate with families of color. For all the talk about educators' efforts to effectively engage parents, Cooper (2009) noted that, when it comes to low income and families of color, "educators typically do not welcome, expect, or cultivate power sharing practices with students' families" (p. 380). Cooper further concluded that "middle-class, white parents are more likely to be perceived as caring parents. African American parents, however, are not cast in such a positive light, nor do they enjoy as much racial privilege" (p. 381).

Despite Mr. Cox's insistence that Principal Donlea reveal who called DHS, she refuses, knowing that this must remain strictly confidential. As he continues to press, the meeting reveals another issue with which schools often struggle: the intersection of race/ethnicity, class, culture and speech. Citing Kochman (1982), Hecht, Ribeau, and Alberts (2004, p. 106) noted that "contrary to the assumption that Afro-Americans and whites share identical speech and cultural conventions, Kochman described differing norms and social styles, pointing to divergent patterns of intonation, expressive intensity, spontaneity, aggressiveness, and argument." According to Baugh (2004) many black Americans face a frequent Catch-22 related to speaking and communication: " . . . although they grew up around peers who value the dialect, when they enter professional society, another style of speaking is demanded" (p. 90).

Ostensibly, Mr. Cox came to school demanding to know who called DHS. As Principal Donlea works through Mr. Cox's outrage, she finds herself wrestling with a complicated array of issues including confidentiality, culture and language, emotion, the law, and office decorum.

THE TRANSCRIPT

Principal:	Good Morning.
Dad:	How're ya doing?
Principal:	I'm Deb Donlea. Nice to meet you.
Dad:	Deb Donlea, right?
Principal:	Yes.
Dad:	Are you the one who called DHS?
Principal:	I'm sorry . . .

Dad:	Who in the hell called DHS?
Principal:	Would you like to sit down so we can . . .
Dad:	Someone called DHS on me. They've been around my house and snooping around . . . and it's full of shit, you know?
Principal:	Ok.
Dad:	It's full of shit. This is full of shit.
Principal:	Okay, well, I tell you what, Mr. Cox
Dad:	You know my son, right?
Principal:	Yes, I do. A wonderful child, wonderful child.
Dad:	Uh huh, uh huh. And everyone's been talking to him and everything about, you know, what's going on and this and that. No one has contacted me. You know he had, I guess a little mark, or said, you know, he's been getting whoopings or whatever, this and that. I believe in whoopings but you know what? You guys don't need to call DHS. That's bullshit.
Principal:	Okay. Well, let me first, would you care to sit down and we can discuss this?
Dad:	Why should I sit down? It's bullshit.
Principal:	Well, I think if we sit down we can calmly talk about it as adults . . .
Dad:	Calmly talk about it? Oh! DHS is not at your fucking house. They're at my house. They're not at your house, ok?
Principal:	Ok. Alright. Well . . .
Dad:	My son is happy. Don't you think so?
Principal:	Yes, he's a wonderful boy. He is a very happy young man.
Dad:	Ok, ok, ok, so what's the problem?
Principal:	Well, I tell you, I'm not exactly sure about . . .
Dad:	So who called?
Principal:	You know, and let me tell you this, Mr. Cox, in a situation like this, ah, we are mandatory reporters as a school . . .
Dad:	I understand that shit . . . I read the fucking rules! I read them, but at the end of the day, you guys don't need to call DHS. I didn't get no call. Why didn't you call and say "is there something wrong?" You make me look like I'm a damn monster. I'm no fucking monster. I'm pissed.
Principal:	I understand that, sir. And no, we don't think that you are a monster.
Dad:	Oh yes you do. Well, DHS is around my house, not yours.
Principal:	As mandatory reporters, we do have to . . . even if there is . . .
Dad:	Oh, there goes the fucking rule again, there goes the fucking rule again. I understand that fucking rule, you need to move on. Who called DHS?
Principal:	That is something that is confidential and DHS has to talk with about you about that.

Dad: Well, why don't you call them up? Call them up. Call them up right now. I want you to call them up and I want you . . . we can all sit down and see if I'm this abuser.

Principal: Ok, sir. I am not going to call DHS at this point. And we've got a couple choices here.

Dad: What are the choices?

Principal: The choices could be that you and I could sit down and calmly talk about this or we could make . . .

Dad: I haven't invaded your space. Have I invaded your space?

Principal: No, you have not. But the tone that you're using with me is not . . .

Dad: The tone? Is your secretary . . . am I talking a little too loud?

Principal: But you are using profanity and I do not wish for the students and the other people in this building to hear this. We are a school and we do have to set a good example for the children . . . so I would be more than happy to . . .

Dad: This is A and B. Don't you think this is an A and B conversation? This is an adult situation.

Principal: Yes it is.

Dad: If you was in my situation, what would you do?

Principal: I would probably talk with the DHS person that has been in contact with you and I understand that you are upset. I do understand that, but please understand that we have to go with suspicion. And in this situation, I'm sure and knowing your child and he is a wonderful young man and you seem like a very nice gentleman yourself . . .

Dad: Huh. Not now.

Principal: But we have to . . .

Dad: What I mean, you still, you know what? Here goes, this is the thing that bugs me. You're a mandatory reporter, correct? Alright. Anything leading up to this point, I'm not getting no phone calls. He's getting good grades. Everything is working fine. He's not acting like he's some abused kid. But you know what? DHS is around my house asking questions, and you know what? Excuse my language, it's bullshit.

Principal: If I don't do my job and if my teachers don't do their job and do report any sort of suspicion, any sort of abuse, whether it's . . . we are liable and we could lose our job. We are here for the children. We want to do what's in the best interest for them. And you know there are times I'm sure when they don't find anything . . . anything that is wrong. But we have to look out for the kids. They are with us seven to eight hours a day.

Dad: That's all about interpretation, isn't it?

Principal: Well, we have to . . .

Dad:	Isn't it?
Principal:	We have to . . .
Dad:	I would like to sit down with all the teachers, counselor and whatever. Let's ask to see who called DHS, because it's all about interpretation. Don't you think so?
Principal:	Could be, but we're . . . at this point it doesn't really matter who called DHS. What matters is we need to get it solved . . .
Dad:	You're right about that. You're right about that one. You're right about that. It doesn't matter. You know why? Cause I'm the one going through hell. I'm the one going through the shit but you know what? You guys are off on your little ivory mountain there and you know what? I have to answer to some allegations that are false. I was raised with a few little whoopings. And you know what? I'm gonna raise my son the same damn way. And if you guys think it's abuse, you know what? You guys don't get it. You really don't get it.

DISCUSSION AND REFLECTION QUESTIONS

1. Identify the key issue(s).
2. Identify the secondary issue(s).
3. Mr. Cox sets an aggressive tone in this scenario, asking immediately (15:57) "Who in the hell called (the Department of Human Services) DHS" adding that "it's full of shit." Should Principal Donlea immediately move to redirect his language? Should she advise Mr. Cox that he will be asked to leave if he continues to use profanity? Or should she simply listen and explore the issues he raises? Justify your position.
4. Mr. Cox acknowledges that he uses "whoopings" do discipline his son. He also says his son is happy and the principal agrees, noting that he is "a wonderful boy and a very happy young man." Mr. Cox then asks, (17:04) "So what's the problem?" Given that the school has reported a possible case of child abuse, how should the principal respond?

   Principal Donlea explains the school's role as a mandatory reporter for possible child abuse. Mr. Cox says he understands that policy and asks why the school didn't call him directly and inquire if there was a problem (17:39). Is this a reasonable question? How should the principal respond?
5. After demanding to know who placed the call and more profanity from Mr. Cox, Principal Donlea begins to offer Mr. Cox two choices for how to proceed. The (18:44) first is to sit down and "calmly talk about this." She never quite gets to the second option, because she addresses

Mr. Cox's use of profanity and the level of his voice. Has she waited too long to explain that she does not want other employees or students to hear Mr. Cox's language? Or, by allowing him to express his frustration, has she shown herself as being willing to listen and that she is not intimidated?

6. At 19:30 Principal Donlea asks Mr. Cox to "please understand that we have to go with suspicion," trying to get Mr. Cox to understand the school's legal and ethical responsibility to protect children. Since she has previously said that Mr. Cox's son appears to be a wonderful happy boy, does her use of the word "suspicion" seem problematic? Does this send the message that she believes Mr. Cox has abused his son?

7. At 19:39 the principal again notes that Mr. Cox's son is a wonderful young man and that Mr. Cox seems like "a very nice gentleman." Evaluate.

8. Mr. Cox complains that he has received no communication from the school regarding potential concerns about his son or possible abuse until a formal call to DHS was made. Is this a valid complaint?

9. At 20:45 Mr. Cox suggests that the issue is related to different interpretations of discipline, corporal punishment, etc. He asks the principal, "It's all about interpretation, isn't it?" Given that some research has concluded that some racial/ethnic and socioeconomic groups are more likely to use corporal punishment than others, does Mr. Cox have a valid point? How should the principal respond?

10. When the principal tells Mr. Cox that it doesn't matter who called DHS, he argues that the investigation allows the school to go on about its business, while he is left to "answer to some allegations that are false." What are the practical implications for a parent/family under investigation for possible child abuse?

11. At 21:38 Mr. Cox notes that he was raised with "a few little whoop-ings" and that he intends to raise his son the same way. He says that if school officials view this as abuse, they "just don't get it." How should the principal respond? Is there a way Principal Donlea can understand Mr. Cox's rights as a parent while helping him understand the school's legal responsibilities?

12. Identify areas in which you believe the principal acted effectively.

13. Identify areas in which you believe the principal could have acted more effectively.

Balcony View

Generally speaking, how did the principal perform in this scenario? What would you have done differently?

Standards In Action

Which standards do you see as relevant in the scenario? Does the principal effectively meet them? Are there standards and/or criteria left unmet by the principal's actions?

Self Check

Picturing yourself in the principal's chair, describe your emotions. Does the case touch any of your biases or prior experiences?

Switch It Up

How might your thinking or approach change if the gender, social class, ethnicity, language, age, sexual orientation or other descriptors of the players involved were different?

Principal's Presence

In televised presidential debates, "looking presidential" is an important measure of a candidate's performance. The same is true for principals. Halpern and Lubar (2003, p. 3) define leadership presence as being more than "commanding attention" to include "the ability to connect authentically with the thoughts and feelings of others." Does the principal exert an effective "Principal's Presence?" Explain.

Principal's Priority

How *serious* is the situation?
How *soon* should the principal address this situation?
Should the principal inform/involve a *supervisor* on this issue?

In A Word

Capture the principal's performance in the scenario using one word.

Collaborate

Collaborate with a classmate or colleague to rewrite or alter the case with a different set of circumstances. Share your new case with other colleagues to ascertain how they would approach it.

Extension & Internship Experiences

- What is your school or district policy related to potential or suspected child abuse? Do teachers, administrators, counselors, and support staff receive training on how to handle concerns, reporting protocol, etc.? Mr. Cox raises the issue of child abuse and interpretation. What do mandatory reporting laws in your state require of educators?
- Does your building designate a particular person to make such reports to the responsible agency in your state? Interview the official charged with responding to issues of this type.
- No principal likes to be caught off guard, especially with an irate stakeholder like Mr. Cox. Does your school or district have an established protocol for informing administrators that a concern has been reported? What school officials will be aware that reports have been made?

REFERENCES AND RESOURCES

Abrams, L. S., & Gibbs, J. T. (2002). Disrupting the logic of home-school relations: Parent involvement strategies and practices of inclusion and exclusion. *Urban Education, 37*(3), 384–440.

Baugh, J. (2004). Black street speech: Its history, structure, and survival. In Jackson II (Ed.) *African American communication and identities: Essential readings* (pp. 89–101). Thousand Oaks, CA: Sage. (Reprinted from *Black street speech: Its history, structure, and survival,* pp. 1–22, by J. Baugh, 1983, Austin, TX: University of Texas Press)

Cooper, C. W. (2009). Parent involvement, African American mothers and the politics of educational care. *Equity and Excellence in Education, 42*(4), 379–394.

De Gaetano, Y. (2007). The role of culture in engineering Latino parents' involvement in school. *Urban Education, 42*(2), 145–162.

Dunklee, D. R., & Shoop, R. J. (2006). *The principal's quick-reference guide to school law: Reducing liability, litigation, and other potential legal tangles.* (2nd ed.). Thousand Oaks, CA: Corwin Press.

Fine, M. (1993). Parent involvement: Reflections on parents, power, and urban public schools. *Teachers College Record, 94*(4), 682–708.

Giles-Sims, J., Straus, M. A., & Sugarman, D. B. (1995). Child, maternal, and family characteristics associated with spanking. *Family Relations, 44*(2), 70–176.

Grogan-Kaylor, A., & Otis, M. D. (2007). The predictors of parental use of corporal punishment. *Family Relations, 56*(1), 80–91. doi: 10.1111/j.1741-3729.2007.00441.x

Hecht, M. L., Jackson II, R. L., & Ribeau, S. A. (2003). *African American communication: Exploring identity and culture.* Manwah, NJ: Lawrence Erlbaum Associates.

Hecht, M. L., Ribeau, S., & Alberts, J. K. (2004). An Afro-American perspective on interethnic communication. In Jackson II (Ed.), *African American communication and identities: Essential readings* (pp.105–124). Thousand Oaks, CA: Sage. (Reprinted from An Afro-American perspective on interethnic communication, pp. 385–410, by M. L. Hecht, S. Ribeau, & J. K. Alberts, 1989, *Communication Monographs, 56*)

Henry, M. (1996). *Parent-school collaboration: Feminist organizational structures and school leadership.* Albany, NY: State University of New York Press.

Kochman, T. (1982). *Black and white: Styles in conflict.* Chicago, IL: University of Chicago Press.

McLoyd, V. C., & Smith, J. (2002). Physical discipline and behavior problems in African American, European American, and Hispanic children: Emotional support as a moderator. *Journal of Marriage and Family, 64*(1), 40–53.

Noguera, P. A. (2001). Transforming urban schools through investments in the social capital of parents. In S. Saegart, J. P. Thompson, & M. Warren (Eds.), *Social capital and poor communities* (pp. 189–212). New York, NY: Russell Sage Foundation.

Hot Seat #5

Look What I Found!
(Elementary School)

Ms. Garza serves as the school district's first-ever Latina principal. Recruited because of her approachable reputation and experience with dual language instruction programs, the district was proud of its aggressive and successful recruiting efforts. Heather, an energetic mother of four young children appears unannounced in Principal Garza's office intent on sharing her displeasure with several aspects of the playground.

Sitting in Principal Garza's office with a large bag of dangerous items she claims to have found on the playground, Heather begins quizzing Principal Garza about the playground and recess. She peppers Principal Garza with questions from policy and equipment maintenance to records of injuries. She also informs Principal Garza that she has conducted her own research into playground safety. Her visit presents an opportunity for Principal Garza to address an issue that was far from the reasons she was recruited into her job: the role of recess and the outdoor environment.

"Studies show that playgrounds are a fundamental part of the elementary school curriculum: They enhance children's physical, emotional, social, and intellectual skills" (Olsen, Hudson, & Thompson, 2002, p. 22). A 2010 Gallup survey of principals revealed that "principals overwhelmingly believe recess has a positive impact not only on the development of students' social skills, but also on achievement and learning in the classroom" (Robert Wood Johnson Foundation, 2010, p. 3).

Despite this, a study by the National Program for Playground Safety gave most playgrounds a C+ for supervision, maintenance, and safety (Olsen, Hudson, & Thompson, 2002). These frequent shortcomings account for a staggering amount of playground-related injuries and are a common source of litigation against school districts (Olsen, Hudson, & Thompson, 2008; Frost & Sweeney, 1996).

Whether interested in playgrounds or helping with copying and field trips, volunteers can offer valuable help to schools. Robbins and Alvy (2009) noted that "the principal is in the most effective position to lead the way in taking the initiative" to involve parents and community members as volunteers" (p. 184). At the same time, wise principals know that some would-be volunteers can create more problems than they solve, through disruption, meddling, or failing to understand their role. The task for principals then becomes how (or whether) to use them.

Heather's passion for the elementary school playground and desire to be involved leads Ms. Garza to invite Heather to become involved in the school's safety committee. As the scenario plays out, Principal Garza wonders if inviting Heather to be involved will be a wonderful solution or an unfortunate mistake.

THE TRANSCRIPT

Mom:	Hi, Miss Garza?
Principal:	Hi Heather. How are you?
Mom:	Nice to meet you.
Principal:	Nice to meet you too. Why don't you sit down?
Mom:	Thank you, thank you. Thanks for taking the time . . . the five minutes . . .
Principal:	Sure. How can I help you?
Mom:	Well, first of all, I gotta ask do you know why I'm dressed like this?
Principal:	You . . . are on a safety committee . . .?
Mom:	Very, yeah, close, yeah. Well, any other thoughts?
Principal:	Uh, you were helping out with crosswalks maybe somewhere?
Mom:	Actually, I'm demonstrating because I've kind of had some concerns...what's going on outside your school . . .
Principal:	Uh huh . . .
Mom:	Just let me take this off cause I don't wanna . . . . You know I'm a parent . . . and I have four children under the age of five that . . . my kindergartener will be starting this year and I'm a little concerned about what's happening outside . . . we live right across the school and I know you have three recesses a day and I see your teachers, uh, they're out there in their stilettos, they have their flip flops on and I'm just disappointed in the behavior that's happening out there . . . They're just on their cell phones texting—talking about laws, I have documentation . . . and I

just wanted to know what your thoughts were on the outdoor environment.

Principal: Well, first of all, I'm glad you're here and talking about these concerns you have and I can validate your concerns because your child will be coming to our school next year.

Mom: Well that's a relief!

Principal: But I would like to share some thoughts of how we are coming together and wanting to improve our behaviors outside, not only with staff but with students as well. Currently we are having staff development on the safety issues. We're gathering a safety committee together and I would love for you to be involved. You could be a part of that committee and you could show us some examples of . . .

Mom: Well, I just don't think that's . . . you know . . . I found this last week, ok, a jump rope, right . . . I found this hanging. Do you know each year seventeen children die on playgrounds? And strangulation is the leading cause. So just recently here in our community we just had a strangulation death. This is a major problem. This is just laying out there. I found this on the weekend. And then, wine! I don't know who's drinking out there but there's wine bottles out there. Have you ever stepped on a broken bottle? Because if this thing would be . . . yeah and my condom, I found a condom out there in my bag. So I've been picking up, I've been collecting things . . . I have documentation of what I have found outside! What are you gonna do about this stuff?

Principal: Well that could be part of our safety committee as well . . . maybe . . .

Mom: Isn't that a little late? I mean, come on, this is four . . . evidence right here. These are all things I found on your playground. And in fact, I don't know if you were here when this happened but a kindergartener ran up to Mr. Olsen and said, "Mr. Olsen, what is this?" A kindergartener! If my five year old found this . . . I mean, come on! What kind of school are you running here?

Principal: Well let me assure you that I will be out there to monitor more of this stuff. Now . . .

Mom: When? Yesterday, today, tomorrow?

Principal: Well as soon as we can have our next recess, our next break . . . Uh, in the mornings when we have . . . the kids are arriving to school . . . I don't know if you do notice the parents who are out there helping us . . . Uh, and as long as once we get the safety committee rolling, uh, we can have all this presentation and show them the importance of elevating the safety of our school. As far as the jump rope is concerned, you know we do want to have our kids active out there and that's why we encourage them to use these kinds of equipment. In our school, we haven't had any issues as far as health or accidents or injuries that deal with any of the concerns that you have here. They're all . . .

Mom: Do you know that for a fact?

Principal: Yes Ma'am, we do. We haven't had any concerns . . . or any injuries or anything up to this point.

Mom: Well I read a statistic, I don't know . . . I should tell you . . . And I'm so glad that you're coming into this school and you're excited and making changes but I actually took it upon myself and I started doing research. For the past couple weeks I've been researching this topic and if you just google playgrounds, outdoor . . . go on the google site . . . You know, there are a lot of . . . good information out there. There's some certificate programs that are out there and so I've purchased these books and I've been reading and I'm actually certified as a playground supervisor by the National Program for Playground Safety, so I feel confident that I know my stuff and in fact there is a research study that was done about five years ago in the state of Iowa that not one school had the same injury report form. So I'm really shocked that you have not had any injuries out there. It just blows my mind because 80 percent of the injuries happen on the playground. You know, so I just . . . you know, I've heard this time and time again . . .

Principal: Uh huh . . .

Mom: In the research that I've done . . .

Principal: Right . . . And maybe you can help us to do our own research here on our own campus. You know, I'm so pleased that you have done so much work and you're so involved. We need parents like you in our school. If I can hook you up with our counselor, we can get this committee started and I would be more than impressed if you could be part of that committee so we can resolve all of these issues that we have right now . . .

Mom: I mean, but I want to ask you a serious question. Have you ever spent any time outside observing the children?

Principal: Yes I have.

Mom: You have? How, how much?

Principal: Any time that I have a chance . . . that I'm not in a meeting or not pulled away by a parent, I am out there, yes.

Mom: Well, could you . . . I would like to see your files of your inspection reports of your documentation of . . . your staff . . . Have they all . . . You said you have parents that are out there supervising. Have they been trained? Do they know what they're looking for? Or are you just assuming this is just easy, it's just the playground, anybody can watch children. Or do you really value the outdoor environment, the part of the curriculum?

Principal: Well, as far as the files are concerned, I don't want to share those with you because of the personal and private information that's in there. I wouldn't want any other parent coming in and asking about your child's information either, and I wouldn't share that with them also. Uh, but I . . .

Mom: So you're telling me that . . . I'm so glad, but, I'm wonderful, I'm very happy that you're saying you look through them. But if I would go to your 12 staff, your 15 staff and I would ask them, you know, do you know what's going, you know, where are your boundaries, what are you playground rules, um, what should you be doing, you know . . . If they're out there wearing their stilettos and their flip flops and they don't have the right safety . . . We think this is just first aid, but, you know, I have Kleenexes in here, it says to have Kleenexes . . .

Principal: Right . . .

Mom: Band-Aids, they should have this vest . . . um, clips, pooper scoopers, you know? What . . . I would like to check all your fanny packs in your school and see if there's a consistency with it.

DISCUSSION AND REFLECTION QUESTIONS

1. Identify the key issue(s)
2. Identify the secondary issue(s).
3. Heather expresses a number of concerns related to the school's outdoor environment, ranging from the shoes teachers are wearing at recess to claiming that they are sending text   messages during recess time. After thanking Heather for coming in to express her concerns, Principal Garza begins to explain how the school is "coming together and wanting to improve behaviors outside" with students and staff alike.

    In doing this, does she effectively thank Heather for raising her concerns? Or does she imply to Heather that she agrees there is a problem? Should Principal Garza have asked to see the "documentation" Heather claims to have? By describing the staff development that is underway, does Principal Garza seem to empower Heather without knowing enough about her or the validity of her concerns?

4. At 23:58 Principal Garza describes the newly formed safety committee and says, "I would love for you to be involved."

   Is it a good idea to invite Heather to be involved in such a committee, given her apparent knowledge and interest in these issues? Perhaps it is a way to engage a potential critic as a partner. On the other hand, what if Heather has a reputation of being an impossible critic or simply a nuisance? Does Principal Garza run the risk of inviting every squeaky wheel onto a school committee by extending the invitation to Heather?

5. At 24:07 Heather begins showing a number of items she claims to have found on the playground, asking "What are you gonna do about this stuff?" How should Principal Garza respond? At 25:12, Principal Garza asserts that she "will be out there to monitor more of this stuff." Is she validating the importance of the playground or admitting that she has not provided effective oversight?

6. An experienced school administrator once said "the best public relations a school can have is a good band, winning football team, and a well-maintained building and grounds." Given this bit of folk wisdom, what is the role of the appearance in the school's playground and outdoor spaces?

7. At 25:14 Principal Garza commits to being "out there to monitor more of this stuff." Is that an admission that there are problems on the playground and that she and the school have not done an effective job of monitoring and maintaining the space? Or does it simply show that she takes Heather's concerns seriously? Assuming that Principal Garza's schedule is already highly demanding, is this a promise she should make? Is that additional time on the playground and outdoor space a wise use of her time? Why or why not?

8. At 26:40 Heather explains that she has conducted research into playground issues and has become certified as a Playground Supervisor by the National Program for Playground Safety. Does this make Principal Garza's invitation to serve on the school safety committee seem more or less appropriate?

9. After asking Principal Garza how much time she spends observing children on the playground, Heather asks to see the school's inspection reports, etc. Is this a reasonable request? Is she entitled to see these documents? How should Principal Garza respond?

10. Heather further presses Principal Garza about the level of training, if any, that staff and/or parents on the playground receive. Are teachers, staff, and volunteers at your school provided training for playground supervision?

11. At 29:05, Heather says she would like to check the school's fanny packs to see if necessary items are included. Is this asking for trouble or a potential way to turn Heather from a critic into part of the solution?

12. How should Principal Garza bring closure to the meeting?
13. Identify areas in which you believe the principal acted effectively.
14. Identify areas in which you believe the principal could have acted more effectively.

Balcony View

Generally speaking, how did the principal perform in this scenario? What would you have done differently?

Standards In Action

Which standards do you see as relevant in the scenario? Does the principal effectively meet them? Are there standards and/or criteria left unmet by the principal's actions?

Self Check

Picturing yourself in the principal's chair, describe your emotions. Does the case touch any of your biases or prior experiences?

Switch It Up

How might your thinking or approach change if the gender, social class, ethnicity, language, age, sexual orientation or other descriptors of the players involved were different?

Principal's Presence

In televised presidential debates, "looking presidential" is an important measure of a candidate's performance. The same is true for principals. Halpern and Lubar (2003, p. 3) define leadership presence as being more than "commanding attention" to include "the ability to connect authentically with the thoughts and feelings of others." Does the principal exert an effective "Principal's Presence?" Explain.

Principal's Priority

How *serious* is the situation?
How *soon* should the principal address this situation?
Should the principal inform/involve a *supervisor* on this issue?

In A Word

Capture the principal's performance in the scenario using one word.

Collaborate

Collaborate with a classmate or colleague to rewrite or alter the case with a different set of circumstances. Share your new case with other colleagues to ascertain how they would approach it.

Extension & Internship Experiences

- What records does your school or district keep regarding playground maintenance and injuries? Conduct a review of those files, noting any action or concerns.
- Conduct a walk through examination of your school's playground/outdoor space, noting any concerns.
- Does your school or district have a person designated to conduct safety and maintenance inspections of the playground and outdoor environment? Given increasing demands on principal's time, is this something that could/ should be designated to someone else? Or is this a key function of the principal? Why or why not? Interview a principal or director of elementary education on their view of the principal's role in this area.
- Research the laws in your state related to playground supervision.

REFERENCES AND RESOURCES

Burris, K. G., & Boyd, F. B. (2005). *Outdoor learning and play, Ages 8–12*. Portland, OR: Association for Childhood Education International.

Clements, R. L. (Ed.). (2000). *Elementary school recess: Selected readings, games, and activities for teachers and parents*. Boston, MA: American Press.

Consumer Product Safety Commission (CPSC) (2011). *Handbook for public playground safety*. Washington, DC: U.S. Government Printing Office.

Frost, J. L., Brown, P. S., Sutterby, J. A., & Thornton, C. D. (2004). *The developmental benefits of playgrounds*. Olney, MD: Association for Childhood Education International.

Frost, J. L., & Sweeney, T. B. (1996). *Cause and prevention of playground injuries and litigation: Case studies*. Wheaton, MD: Association for Childhood Education International.

Kutska, K. S., Hoffman, K. J., & Malkuska, A. (1998). *Playground safety is no accident: Developing a public playground safety and maintenance program.*(2nd ed.). Ashburn, VA: National Recreation and Park Association.

National Arbor Day Foundation. (2007). *Learning with nature idea book: Creating nurturing outdoor spaces for children.* Lincoln, NE: Author.

Olsen, H., Hudson, S. D., & Thompson, D. (2002, August). Child's play: What your school board should know about playground supervision and safety. *American School Board Journal*, 22–24.

Olsen, H., Hudson, S. D., & Thompson, D. (2008). Developing a playground injury prevention plan. *The Journal of School Nursing, 24*(3), 131–137.

Olsen, H., Hudson, S. D., & Thompson, D. (2010, August). Creating and maintaining elementary school outdoor environments for children in the 2010 decade. *American School Board Journal, 197*(8), 27–29.

Olsen, H., Hudson, S. D., & Thompson, D. (2010, August). State of play. *American School Board Journal, 197*(8), 27–29.

Robert Wood Johnson Foundation. (2010). *The state of play: Gallup survey of principals on school recess.* Princeton, NJ: Author.

Robbins, P., & Alvy, H. B. (2009). *The principal's companion: Strategies for making the job easier.* (3rd ed.). Thousand Oaks, CA: Corwin Press.

Schwebel, D. C. (2006). Safety on the playground: Mechanisms through which adult supervision might prevent child playground injury. *Journal of Clinical Psychology in Medical Settings, 13*(2), 141–149.

Thompson, D., Hudson, S. D., & Olsen, H. (2007). *S.A.F.E. play areas: Creation, maintenance, and renovation.* Champaign, IL: Human Kinetics.

The National Program for Playground Safety offers a host of resources related to playgrounds and recess. Their website is: http://www.uni.edu/playground/

Hot Seat #6

What Are They Doing In There? (Elementary School)

As an applicant for the elementary principalship, one of the first people Dameon Place met was Mr. Stamp, a popular, influential local banker and member of the interview committee. Dameon had been immediately impressed with Mr. Stamp's passion for the school and community. After accepting the job, he appreciated Mr. Stamp's help in securing a mortgage and meeting other influential people in the community. Mr. and Mrs. Stamp had gone out of their way to make Dameon and his family feel welcome, and it was good to know some people not directly associated with the school district.

Mr. Stamp pops into Principal Place's office, concerned that his fifth grade son is struggling in history. To Principal Place's surprise, his new friend believes the root of the problem lies not with his son, the curriculum, or the teacher. Mr. Stamp believes special education students in the class are distracting his son. And he wants his new friend, Principal Place, to fix it.

The number of students served by special education programs has grown significantly since the Individuals with Disabilities Education Act (IDEA) became law in 1975. Miller (2007) cited a government report estimating nearly seven million students receive special education services. As the number of students served has increased, so has the percentage of time special education students spend in regular classrooms. For example, Morrison (2009) noted that 95 percent of special education students spend at least part of their day in regular education classrooms. With a well-established relationship between poverty, language/ethnicity and special education, school leaders must anticipate continued pressure in coming years (Ubben, Hughes, & Norris, 2011).

Despite this growth, many educators remain critical of what school administrators Chesley and Calaluce, Jr. (1997) called "our national obsession with the inclusion of special education students into the mainstream" (p. 488). The authors made an argument that is familiar to many, charging that the current system shortchanges too many special education students in the name of socialization and political correctness, and that parent demands for mainstreaming are "often unrealistic, and at times absurd" (p. 489). The authors also argued that many regular education teachers cannot effectively meet special students' needs in the general education environment, thus leaving them unprepared for life after high school.

Kliewer (1998), however, in a scathing rebuke of Chesley and Calaluce, Jr., dismissed their criticism as an attempt to "misinform, misrepresent, and misapprehend the meaning of inclusion" in addition to "ridiculing parents" (para. 1). Kliewer cited a litany of research that "suggests that inclusion works and works well, for all children when we make it work" (para. 16). Further, he argued, researchers have found again and again that the benefits of inclusion extend to regular education students in terms of social development and a range of academic areas. "In essence, an overwhelming amount of research documents extensive benefits for all children educated in effective inclusive classrooms" (para. 23).

In the 30-plus years since passage of IDEA, educators, parents, and interest groups have toiled with the law's intent and application. Tomlinson's (2003) observation characterized the ongoing debate between the Chesley and Calaluce Jr. and Kliewer perspectives perfectly: "The United States has always balanced precariously on the twin values of equity and excellence" (p. 9).

For Principal Place, the precarious balance appears in the form of Mr. Stamp's call for him to "do something" about those special education kids who are distracting his son. This leaves the principal needing to respond in a way that reflects the law, his philosophy, and educators' moral and ethical responsibilities to all students.

THE TRANSCRIPT

Principal:	Hello, Mr. Stamp.
Dad:	Dameon! How's it going, buddy?
Principal:	Good to see you.
Dad:	Good to see you too.
Principal:	Let's have a seat here.

Dad:	Ok.
Principal:	I'll grab my paper.
Dad:	Ok . . .
Principal:	Thanks for coming in.
Dad:	Yeah, you bet. Hey, Dameon, we've got a situation here. I was talking to Michael the other day and he mentioned that in his history class . . . Uh, with Mr. Peterson . . . . there's a couple kids in there that are distracting him from getting his work done. And so I kind of, ah, made an excuse to stop by the classroom the other day and I've gotta tell you, there are a couple of kids in there that shouldn't be in there and I think we've gotta do something.
Principal:	Ok. Ah, what's going on?
Dad:	Well, I don't . . . for Michael, he's doing poorly in history.
Principal:	Ok.
Dad:	Uh, and ah, you know, it's a subject he shouldn't do poorly in, but there's a couple . . . the kids, I don't know their names but, there those special education kids, ok? And they're, there's a couple of them and I was in there, you know, they're making noises and they're drooling and their wheelchairs are hitting other chairs and shit like that . . . I mean, they shouldn't be in there.
Principal:	Ok.
Dad:	I mean, don't you think . . . don't you gotta get them out of there?
Principal:	No, I think they should be there. That's what we do here.
Dad:	Seriously?
Principal:	Yeah, it's, it's kind of a law. We need to include them as much as we can. I understand your concern. I understand Michael's having a hard time with the distractions going on. Ah, what period does he have history?
Dad:	Seventh period, Mr. Peterson.
Principal:	Seventh period. Ah . . .
Dad:	So that's your response? Is it's the law?
Principal:	Well, it's part of my response.
Dad:	Ok, what's the other part?
Principal:	Well, I need to gather a little bit more information, to be honest with you. Ah, how has Michael done in history before? Has he done . . . or, you know, what . . .
Dad:	Well, mostly B's and he's getting a C right now, but you know, it's not just Michael . . .
Principal:	Ok
Dad:	It's all the kids. I mean, why do, I mean . . .
Principal:	Let's focus mainly on Michael, right now . . .

Dad: Well, let's tell you this, if Michael were disrupting the class as much as those kids are disrupting the class, he'd be out of there . . .

Principal: Ok.

Dad: What do you think about that?

Principal: I haven't seen the problem, so I don't know. You know, and that's the thing. I think that what I need to do, ah, Mr. Stamp, is I'd like to stop down, seventh period today actually . . . I'll just, I'll go down and sit through the class with Mr. Peterson and gather a little bit more information. Is it ok if I call you after school today? Perhaps we can sit down with Michael and you and address the situation and get a look at, ah, some of the concerns that you both have regarding his grade and regarding the situation in the class.

Dad: Well, yeah, I suppose, I mean I would expect you're gonna at least do that, to see with your own eyes, and that's all well and good, but really, what are they doing in there?

Principal: They're learning.

Dad: Really?

Principal: Yeah.

Dad: You think they can learn?

Principal: I do.

Dad: Isn't it just a feel good, everyone pretends they can learn, bullshit policy?

Principal: No, it's not. I understand that from the outside you may think that, but that's not what we're doing as public educators. We want to make sure that we try to get every student the best education possible and sometimes it's, and sometimes it's, ah, a difficult situation but we're going to do the best we can for Michael. That's really the main concern here . . . for you.

Dad: Well that is the main concern. So, how . . .

Principal: And for me, the main concern is that all of my students in my building get an excellent education. And that's what I'm gonna do. I'm gonna go down and see Mr. Peterson's class today seventh hour. I'll give you a call after school.

Dad: But how is . . . I understand what you're saying, that everyone has to have a chance to learn. Fine. But, what about Michael? What about his chance? What about his rights? What about my money paying for him to go to this school? I mean, he can, I can go to another school.

Principal: Yes, you can. Yeah, and that's fine. If you'd like to do that, they'll have the same policies that we have regarding that. I'll talk to you after school today. I appreciate you coming in. Thanks a lot.

Dad: Ok. Talk to you then.

DISCUSSION AND REFLECTION QUESTIONS

1. Identify the key issue(s).
2. Identify the secondary issue(s).
3. Judging from the start of this scenario, it appears that the two have met previously and may be on a first name basis. Dameon, the principal, addresses the visitor as "Mr. Stamp." Mr. Stamp addresses Dameon less formally, with "Dameon, how's it going, buddy?"

   Depending on the size of school and community, principals often live in "a fishbowl," being fairly well known in the community. At the same time, virtually every principal can describe the loneliness that comes with some aspects of school leadership. This can be made more complicated by stakeholders who may wish to leverage their relationship with the principal to their or their children's benefit. Practically speaking, how can a principal navigate the complicated path of acting professionally, respecting confidentiality, and telling stakeholders (and friends) things they don't want to hear all while maintaining friendships?
4. At 30:15 Mr. Stamp seems to assume that Principal Place will agree that the special education students in his son's history classroom are a distraction and should be moved. Evaluate Principal Place's response to Mr. Stamp.
5. Mr. Stamp seems unimpressed with Principal Place's response that the presence of special education students in his son's history class is the law. He seems to believe Principal Place is hiding behind the law and begins to discuss other students. At 30:57 Principal Place redirects the conversation to focus on Michael and his performance in history. Mr. Stamp counters and says, "If Michael were disrupting the class as much as those kids are disrupting the class, he'd be out of there. What do you think about that?"

   How should Principal Place respond?

   Principal Place's actual response is "I haven't seen the problem, so I don't know." Evaluate.
6. Mr. Stamp is unsatisfied with the response to the situation, including Principal Place's plan to observe the class. He presses what may be a larger philosophical point, asking what the special education students are doing in the class. Evaluate Principal Place's response.
7. At 32:28 Principal Place sets his note pad and pen on the table, signaling that the meeting is nearing an end. When Mr. Stamp raises Michael's rights and the possibility of them choosing to enroll in another school, Principal Place says, "Yes you can. And that's fine." Evaluate this statement. Does Principal Place seem to dismiss Mr. Stamp's concern or call his bluff, inviting him to choose another school? Or is he simply acknowledging that Mr. Stamp understands his options and is free to enroll his son elsewhere?

8. Would a private school have the same policies?
9. Evaluate the way Principal Place brings closure to the meeting.
10. Identify areas in which you believe the principal acted effectively.
11. Identify areas in which you believe the principal could have acted more effectively.

Balcony View

Generally speaking, how did the principal perform in this scenario? What would you have done differently?

Standards In Action

Which standards do you see as relevant in the scenario? Does the principal effectively meet them? Are there standards and/or criteria left unmet by the principal's actions?

Self Check

Picturing yourself in the principal's chair, describe your emotions. Does the case touch any of your biases or prior experiences?

Switch It Up

How might your thinking or approach change if the gender, social class, ethnicity, language, age, sexual orientation or other descriptors of the players involved were different?

Principal's Presence

In televised presidential debates, "looking presidential" is an important measure of a candidate's performance. The same is true for principals. Halpern and Lubar (2003, p. 3) define leadership presence as being more than "commanding attention" to include "the ability to connect authentically with the thoughts and feelings of others." Does the principal exert an effective "Principal's Presence?" Explain.

Principal's Priority

How *serious* is the situation?
How *soon* should the principal address this situation?
Should the principal inform/involve a *supervisor* on this issue?

In A Word

Capture the principal's performance in the scenario using one word.

Collaborate

Collaborate with a classmate or colleague to rewrite or alter the case with a different set of circumstances. Share your new case with other colleagues to ascertain how they would approach it.

Extension & Internship Experiences

- Principals are often in a position to tell others "no," whether the issue is legal, budgetary or involves judgment. Transitioning from the role of a classroom teacher, this often puts them in an unfamiliar position. How comfortable are you telling people no? Will it be more difficult for you say no to friends and acquaintances than strangers? Does your school or district have a stated policy with regard to mainstreaming special education students?
- What are the applicable laws and policies related to Least Restrictive Environment (LRE)? Interview you principal, director of special education, or other appropriate official to gain insight into how they believe objections like Mr. Stamp's should be addressed.

REFERENCES AND RESOURCES

Chesley, G. M., & Calaluce, Jr., P. D. (1997, Winter). The deception of inclusion. *Mental Retardation, 35*(6), 488–490.

Curry, C. (2003). Universal design: Accessibility for all learners. *Educational Leadership, 61*(2), 55–60.

Greeley, K. (2000). *Why fly that way?: Linking community and academic achievement.* New York, NY: Teachers College Press.

Kliewer, C. (1998). The meaning of inclusion. *Mental Retardation, 36*(4), 317–322.

Miller, G. (2007). Individuals with disabilities act (IDEA) overview. Washington, DC: Committee on Education and Labor; U. S. House of Representatives.

Morrison, G. (2009). *Teaching in America* (5th ed.). Boston, MA: Allyn & Bacon.

Munk, D. D., & Bursuck, W. D. (2003). Grading students with disabilities. *Educational Leadership, 61*(2), 38–43.

Sapon-Shevin, M. (1998). *Because we can change the world: A practical guide to building cooperative, inclusive classroom communities.* Boston, MA: Allyn & Bacon.

Sapon-Shevin, M. (2003). Inclusion: A matter of social justice. *Educational Leadership, 61*(2), 25–28.

Sapon-Shevin, M. (2007). *Widening the circle: The power of inclusive classrooms.* Boston, MA: Beacon Press.

Thomas, G., & Loxley, A. (2008). *Deconstructing special education and constructing inclusion.* Philadelphia, PA: Open University Press.

Tomlinson, C. A. (2003). Deciding to teach them all. *Educational Leadership, 61*(2), 6–11.

Ubben, G. G., Hughes, L. W., & Norris, C. J. (2011). *The principal: Creative leadership for excellence in schools* (7th Ed.).Upper Saddle River, NJ: Pearson.

Hot Seat #7

She Has it Out For All the Athletes! (High School)

Coach Green, a high school social studies teacher and popular basketball coach, has earned a reputation as a passionate advocate for his players. During his tenure at the school, he has increased participation and interest in basketball, while at the same time demanding good behavior from players and carefully monitoring weekly grade checks. While some deride his style as abrasive at times, others respect the way he uses basketball to connect with struggling students and families.

Miss Washington, a high school English teacher and accomplished poet, has also acquired a reputation as a serious teacher who emphasizes student responsibility and accountability. Many of the school's graduates have noted that Miss Washington's classes are more challenging than their freshman English courses in college. Like Coach Green, however, she also has detractors who complain she's overly rigid and who take issue with her assertion that "America is obsessed with sports."

On this Thursday afternoon, Coach Green asks Principal McDonald for help with an eligibility problem. James, a star player and college prospect, received a grade on Miss Washington's English test that will render him ineligible to play in Friday's district championship game. He questions the timing of the test, the pressure she put on James to pass, and what he describes as Miss Washington's unwillingness to help James. He sees the week's events as evidence of her bias against athletes.

Conventional thinking among many educators has long held that student involvement in school activities leads to improved student performance in many areas. Fredricks and Eccles (2006) noted a "growing body of research in leisure studies, sociology, sports psychology and adolescent development demonstrating the beneficial effects of participation in extracurricular activities" (p. 698). A number of scholars (Cooper, Valentine, Nye, & Lindsay, 1999; Eccles & Barber, 1999; Marsh & Kleitman, 2002) have identified a connection between participation and improved educational outcomes, while others have identified desirable connections, such as improved self-esteem (Mahoney, Schweder, & Stattin, 2002) and decreased drop-out rates (Mahoney & Cairns, 1997). Mahoney (2000) contended that the benefits of participation may be especially valuable for at-risk students.

Other researchers have argued that sports have come to occupy too large a role in schools and society. Eitzen and Sage (2009, p. 91) noted that high school athletics have become so important that many schools "appear to an outsider to be more concerned with athletics than with scholarly endeavors." Some have argued that assumed benefits of extracurricular involvement may be overstated or that involvement may be associated with negatives, such as increased alcohol use (Eccles & Barber, 1999) and higher levels of anxiety (Fredricks et al., 2002).

Coakley (2007, p. 485) noted that differences between athletes' and non-athletes' grade point averages, attitudes toward school, absenteeism, and other commonly identified factors associated with participation in sports "have been modest" and that "it has been difficult for researchers to separate the effects of sports participation from the effects of social class, family background, support from friends, identity issues, and other factors related to educational attitudes and achievement." Coakley (p. 484) also concluded that both sides "often exaggerate the benefits or the problems associated with interscholastic sports. Supporters emphasize glowing success stories, and critics emphasize shocking cases of abuse, but the most accurate descriptions probably lie somewhere in the middle."

Principal McDonald faces a dilemma involving two respected teachers, a "good kid," and the role of athletics in high school. And the clock is running.

THE TRANSCRIPT

Principal:	How're you doing?
Coach:	Heather, I've been better, to be honest with you.
Principal:	What's happening?
Coach:	We've got a bit of a situation that you're probably not aware of. Our star basketball player, James Hill, and you may or may not be aware of this too . . . We have a district championship game Friday night and you haven't been to a game all year, so you may not be aware of that. But Tuesday in Miss Washington's class, ah, she came to him and said, "If you don't pass this test, get a

C or better, you're gonna be ineligible for the game on Friday."
Everybody knows Miss Washington has it out for athletes. You
know, she's mad because nobody cares about the haiku or Ralph
Waldo Emerson and everybody cares about how the football team
does or how the basketball team does on Friday. Well, this is the
biggest game we've had at this school in fifteen years. And without James, we're not gonna win the championship. So, he takes
the test on Tuesday. She doesn't give him any warning other than
right before the test, "Hey, you've gotta pass this test, get a C or
better, or you're not gonna be eligible." James panics, doesn't do
well on the test. He came to me in tears and we've got a couple
other things that play in to this . . . It's not just about the team and
him not being able to play on Friday . . . certainly we need him
to win. But it's about the fact that if he doesn't pass this class, he
can't get that college scholarship. And the only way he's going
to college . . . you know, cause as soon as I got done talking to
James, mom called me. Mom was in a panic and said, "Hey,
James' only chance to go to college and get out of this situation
we're in here as a family is through an athletic scholarship." And
we've got two coaches coming in to watch the game Friday. We
don't win the game, we don't get to play another game. So the
fact that James might be eligible on Monday doesn't do us any
good. He needs to be eligible to play on Friday. And if he plays
in the game on Friday and we win, his opportunities for college,
his opportunities to get out of the situation he's in are right there
in front of him. She doesn't care. And everybody knows she
has it out for athletes. She's had it out for athletes all 10 years
I've been here. And she doesn't care. You know, I went to her
directly and said, "Hey, can James do anything, can we get him a
tutor, how can we help him through this process . . . " "He's just
like any other student to me." That's all she said. And it's really
frustrating as not only a teacher but as a coach that I have to deal
with this kind of stuff when we've got our biggest game of the
year. You know, and I want to be at practice, which started five
minutes ago and my assistant started it. I waited out there for ten
minutes to get in here to see you. It's extremely frustrating. And
I want to know what's going to be done now, so he's able to play
on Friday.

Principal: So, he didn't do very well on the test and she told him if he did
not get an A, what would happen?

Coach: If he didn't get a C or better . . .

Principal: C or better . . .

Coach: If he didn't get a C, he wouldn't be able to play on Friday.
Because the school policy is, you know, you've gotta be eligible

in all your classes when they do the grade checks in order to be eligible to play in the game. Well, he's eligible in all his other classes but he's not eligible in this class cause he's got an F right now in this class, ok? Ah, and so, you know, understanding that's school policy, I want to know what can we do to get him to be able to play in this game so that he doesn't miss out on all these opportunities. Without this scholarship, without him playing this game, those opportunities don't exist.

Principal: And you did say that you went to her and asked her to give him a tutor?

Coach: I did. I went to her, but it was a waste of time. I knew it would be. You know, she didn't have time for me. And it's not really my fight. It's James' fight and I understand that . . . and his mom. And James went to her too, that's where he went to first, but she didn't want to deal with James either.

Principal: Well, I think we're kind of at an impasse, a little bit, because um, I mean, you did go and talk to her, but that's my question, I guess. Did James go and talk to her?

Coach: He talked to her. Yep, he did. Absolutely. The minute he got the test.

Principal: And how did that conversation go?

Coach: As I said, she's not gonna do anything. She said he's just like any other student . . . so he can't, I'm not gonna do anything to help him that I wouldn't do for any other student. So what she's telling me is that she must not be willing to help anybody.

Principal: Is James over at practice . . . right now?

Coach: He's at practice but that's not going to do us any good, cause he can't play in the game. I gotta know what's gonna happen cause these college recruiters are flying to see the game and they fly in and say, "Where's James?' Ah, you know, he's not eligible . . . Red flag, no scholarship. He's out of luck.

Principal: Um . . .

Coach: James is pumping gas like his two older brothers who couldn't get eligible.

Principal: And I am concerned about that, I mean I feel like James has real potential . . . he can probably play ball in college and things like that, but I guess what I'm concerned about is that, um, first of all, well, let me ask this first, I guess, did the mom or the parents ask . . . find out about a tutor or did they contact the teacher or anything like that?

Coach: Ah, no. To my knowledge, because James just found out that he was worried . . . that he needed to pass this class on Tuesday when he took the test.

Principal: Oh, I'm sure James knew throughout the trimester or semester that he was not doing fine in the class . . .

Coach: Well, I don't know how she communicates because this isn't a problem just with my athletes, it's a problem with all the athletes. She seems to have it out for them. So whether or not they did or not, I guess I don't know that. My fear is what's going to happen to him in the next two days. And you know, mom is panicked and I . . . I'm not gonna go to mom and say "he can't play Friday." Somebody else has got to tell her. Cause I can't do that to them. She's gonna be outraged and she's gonna want answers as to why this is the case.

Principal: Well, I think, um, maybe we need to talk to . . . or I need to talk to the teacher . . . um, and see. I'm not saying that I'm really delighted about the idea that a coach has come in here asking me to break a school rule for one student. I don't think that's something we want to open that door and set that precedence . . . and although I am concerned about James, I guess I just feel like, you know, where were his parents, you know, a couple weeks ago even, um, and I know you're telling me that you went and talked to the teacher and this is the first I've heard of it and unfortunately, if you would have come to me right after you talked to her and said, "look, this is my concern about James, she has not, I'm trying to get him a tutor, she has not even remotely interested in helping him out to pass English," I, you know, that would be something I needed to know a couple weeks ago and not right now. I'm just not sure . . .

Coach: Didn't know about it a couple weeks ago, otherwise I would have come to you. You're absolutely right. If I'd have known about it two weeks ago, we wouldn't have this problem. But every week, we do these grade checks and he's fine, he's fine, he's fine . . . Oh! District championship. Oh! James is ineligible.

Principal: Well, when did these conversations happen then about the tutor . . . is what I'm asking.

Coach: Wednesday. The test was Tuesday, got the results Wednesday, game is tomorrow, which is Friday. I'm here right now. I mean, as quickly as I can act with still trying to coach my team, teach my classes and do everything else, you know . . . and . . .

Principal: So you were asking about a tutor after he had already failed the test?

Coach: What can I do, yeah. Tutor, make up work, anything. I'm just trying to work with her to work with James.

Principal: Well then you know as well as I do that it's too late then.

Coach: Well, we've got . . . I understand your needing . . . can't change the rule . . . I'm not asking you to change the rule. I'm asking you to look at this situation and James . . . He's been a model citizen, never been in trouble, you know, represented our school since he

was a sophomore on the varsity basketball team and hasn't been
in trouble in any of his classes . . . Here he is, a chance to go to
college and she's gonna blow it all up cause . . . she doesn't think
he . . . you know, he didn't pass this test all of the sudden right
before the district championship.

DISCUSSION AND REFLECTION QUESTIONS

1. Identify the key issue(s).
2. Identify the secondary issue(s).
3. Early in the scenario (33:23) Coach Green notes that Principal McDonald
   has not been to a basketball game all year. Is this appropriate? Does he
   have a reason to expect the principal to attend basketball games? Is it
   appropriate to raise the issue in this way? Would you respond to his
   comment? As principal, what will be/are your intentions for attending
   extra-curricular activities? Will you/have you communicated those
   intentions to sponsors, coaches, and students?
4. At 33:37 Coach Green says, "Everybody knows Miss Washington has
   it out for athletes . . . she's mad because nobody cares about the haiku
   or Ralph Waldo Emerson and everybody cares about how the football
   team does or the basketball team does on Friday." Is it appropriate for
   him to level this charge against Miss Washington? Do you interpret his
   comment about haiku and Emerson as disrespect of Miss Washington
   and her program or simply frustration? Should Principal McDonald
   respond?
5. Part of Coach Green's complaint seems to be that James found out just
   before taking the test on Tuesday that he needed a C or better on the test
   to be eligible to play on Friday. Does he have a reasonable argument
   that this impacted James' performance on the test and that his score
   making him ineligible so close to the championship game on Friday is
   unfair?

   Assuming Miss Washington refused to provide James assistance that
   was any different from what other students might receive, does Coach
   Green have a legitimate complaint? How should a principal decide between strict adherence to policy and exercising judgment and flexibility
   for the good of an individual?
6. At 37:25 Principal McDonald says she's sure James knew his grade in
   the class before the test. Coach Green counters that he does not know
   how Miss Washington communicates and what James knew, but insists
   that these issues are not unique to the players on his team. Most teachers

are dedicated professionals with students' best interests in mind. They are also human. Assume that Miss Washington is perceived by some teachers, parents, and students to "have it in" for athletes. What might be done in a situation in which a teacher is perceived by some to have a vendetta against a particular group of students? What if Coach Green had come with a group of coaches and extra-curricular sponsors who all expressed the same concern about Miss Washington?

7. At 38:30 Principal McDonald questions why issues surrounding James' grades weren't raised two weeks before and that this is the first she has heard of the situation. What is an appropriate role for the principal to play in matters like these? We know that involved families are very important, yet levels of parental involvement differ. What if James' mother holds the view that her job is to provide a home for James and the school's job is to educate him?

8. Coach Green counters that weekly grade checks indicated that James' grade in English was fine and that he did not know about the issues until after the test on Tuesday. If Miss Washington has not entered or recorded grades for several weeks, is his claim more legitimate?

9. At 39:23 Principal McDonald says that since the tutor was not discussed until after the test on Tuesday " . . . You know as well as I do, it's too late . . ." In your opinion, is this an example of the principal enforcing the policy and allowing James to experience the consequences of becoming ineligible? Or is it a case of acting too rigidly and not looking closely enough for a way for James to be eligible to play?

   If Principal McDonald decides to find a way for James to become eligible to play, is she acting unethically? Or is she acting with the best interests of a student who stands to benefit from some flexibility and discretion on the part of the principal and teachers?

10. Principal McDonald said she is not comfortable with a coach asking her to break a school rule for one student. Coach Green counters that he understands the rule and is not asking her to break it, but rather look at James' situation. How should teachers address policies they believe are ill-conceived? How should principals deal with policies they believe are ill-conceived?

11. If Principal McDonald chose to investigate Coach Green's claim that Miss Washington has a bias against athletes, what data might she examine?

12. Regardless of the way Principal McDonald chooses to handle this situation, what might she do in the future to avoid a similar situation?

13. If James is held ineligible by the school, does he have any legal recourse? Would it be unethical for Coach Green to encourage James' family

to pursue legal avenues? If he did, how should Principal McDonald respond?

14. Identify areas in which you believe the principal acted effectively.
15. Identify areas in which you believe the principal could have acted more effectively.

Balcony View

Generally speaking, how did the principal perform in this scenario? What would you have done differently?

Standards In Action

Which standards do you see as relevant in the scenario? Does the principal effectively meet them? Are there standards and/or criteria left unmet by the principal's actions?

Self Check

Picturing yourself in the principal's chair, describe your emotions. Does the case touch any of your biases or prior experiences?

Switch It Up

How might your thinking or approach change if the gender, social class, ethnicity, language, age, sexual orientation or other descriptors of the players involved were different?

Principal's Presence

In televised presidential debates, "looking presidential" is an important measure of a candidate's performance. The same is true for principals. Halpern and Lubar (2003, p. 3) define leadership presence as being more than "commanding attention" to include "the ability to connect authentically with the thoughts and feelings of others." Does the principal exert an effective "Principal's Presence?" Explain.

Principal's Priority

How *serious* is the situation?
How *soon* should the principal address this situation?
Should the principal inform/involve a *supervisor* on this issue?

In A Word

Capture the principal's performance in the scenario using one word.

Collaborate

Collaborate with a classmate or colleague to rewrite or alter the case with a different set of circumstances. Share your new case with other colleagues to ascertain how they would approach it.

Extension & Internship Experiences

- Some would argue that the entire situation should be handled by the activities director rather than the principal. Yet it is easy to see how the issue involves the principal. What is the division of responsibility for these issues at your school or district?
- What is your school or district policy related to extracurricular eligibility? Are there also conference or state requirements? Who has the ultimate responsibility for checking grades and communicating about student progress? Interview a principal or activities director around these issues. Review the rules and determine if there are holes in the reporting procedures, timing, redress of concerns, etc. Are these communicated to parents and students through a handbook and/or meetings?
- In your school or district, are teachers required to maintain current grades for the purpose of determining eligibility? How does this work for teachers who collect few daily or weekly grades and instead employ large test or project grades periodically?

REFERENCES AND RESOURCES

Coakley, J. (2007). *Sports in society: Issues and controversies.* (9th ed.). Boston, MA: McGraw Hill.

Cooper, H., Valentine, J. C., Nye, B., & Lindsay, J. J. (1999). Relationships between five after-school activities and academic achievement. *Journal of Educational Psychology, 9,* 369–378.

Cushman, K. (2006). Help us care enough to learn. *Educational Leadership, 63*(5), 34–7

Darling, N. (2004). Participation in extracurricular activities and adolescent adjustment: Cross-sectional and longitudinal findings. *Journal of Youth and Adolescence, 34*(5), 493–505.

Eccles, J. S., & Barber, B. L. (1999). Student council, volunteering, basketball, or marching band: What kind of extracurricular involvement matters? *Journal of Adolescent Research, 10,* 10–43.

Edwards, R., Smokowskia, P., Sowers, K, B., Dulmus, C. N., & Theriot, M. T. (2005). Abuse of power: When school personnel bully students. *Journal of Evidence-Based Social Work, 1*(2–3), 111–129.

Eitzen, D. D. & Sage, G. H. (2009). *The sociology of North American sport.* (8th ed.). Boulder, CO: Paradigm Publishers.

Fredricks, J. A., & Eccles, J. S. (2006). Is extracurricular participation associated with beneficial outcomes? Concurrent and longitudinal relations. *Developmental Psychology, 42*, 698–713.

Fredricks, J. A., Alfeld-Liro, C., Eccles, J. S., Hruda, L. Z., Patrick, H., & Ryan, A. M. (2002). A qualitative exploration of adolescents' commitment to athletics and the arts. *Journal of Adolescent Research, 17*, 68–97.

Holloway, J. H. (1999, December/2000, January). Extracurricular activities: The path to academic success? *Educational Leadership, 57*(4), 87–88.

Mahoney, J. L. (2000). School extracurricular activity participation as a moderator in the development of antisocial patterns. *Child Development, 71*, 502–516.

Mahoney, J., & Cairns, R. (1997). Do extracurricular activities protect against early school dropout? *Developmental Psychology, 33*, 241–25.

Mahoney, J. L., Schweder, A. E., & Stattin, H. (2002). Structured after-school activities as a moderator of depressed mood for adolescents with detached relations to their parents. *Journal of Community Psychology, 30*, 69–86.

Marsh, H. W., & Kleitman, S. (2002). Extracurricular school activities: The good, the bad, and the non-linear. *Harvard Educational Review, 72*, 464–514.

Reeves, D. R. (2008, September). The extracurricular advantage. *Educational Leadership, 66*(1), 86–87.

Reis, S. M., Colbert, R. D., & Hebert, T. P. (2005). Understanding resilience in diverse, talented students in an urban high school. *Roeper Review, 27*(2), 110–120.

Roberts, J. (2007, December). A sane island surrounded. *Phi Delta Kappan, 89*(4), 278–282.

Staffo, D. F. (1991, April/May). The principal can help keep athletics in proper perspective. *The High School Journal, 74*, 181–185.

Hot Seat #8

It's Time for Them to Go
(Middle School)

It is October of Principal O'Donnell's first year in the middle school when Dr. Lindaman, the Associate Superintendent for Human Resources, stops by her office. Dr. Lindaman has earned a reputation as a no-nonsense administrator with high expectations and a direct communication style. Her intense focus on accountability has produced an enthusiastic group of followers, along with some detractors. Supporters sing her praises, noting they always know right where they stand, while others fear getting caught on her bad side. "Once you're in her crosshairs, it's over," they say.

On this fall afternoon, Dr. Lindaman informs Principal O'Donnell that she has decided time has run out for three middle school teachers. She says their negative attitudes over several years have had a significant impact on the school's culture and climate, and they show no signs of changing. While Dr. Lindaman never uses the word "termination," it is clear that she does not want to see them continue as teachers in the district. Dr. Lindaman's position leaves Principal O'Donnell trying to find a balance between her own style, forming her own opinions about staff, and not alienating the associate superintendent.

Few topics today generate more attention than teacher quality. From educational journals and texts devoted exclusively to instructional leadership to popular media such as *Newsweek* and the evening news, demands for better teaching abound. Debate rages about whether the focus should be on improving current teachers and the systems in which they work or ferreting out underperformers.

In their widely publicized *Newsweek* cover story, Thomas and Wingert (2010) noted that "many principals don't even try to weed out the poor performers (or they transfer them to other schools in what's been dubbed the 'dance of the lemons')" (para. 6). Others, such as Whitaker (2003) have argued that "most teachers do the best they know how" and "if we want them to do better, we must help them improve their skills and master new ones" (p. 35). Either way, principals bear significant responsibility for the quality of instruction students' experience.

While the "dance of the lemons" has received considerable attention in both the literature and popular media, mistreatment of teachers by school administrators has flown largely under the radar. Blase (2009) noted that while workplace abuse across many fields has been widely studied, research into school administrator mistreatment of teachers is very limited. A full 70 percent of teachers in a study by Blase, Blase, and Du (2008) reported extended periods of abuse by school administrators. Jazzar and Algozzine (2007, p. 154) cautioned that "professional disagreements between educational leaders and those they lead do not constitute sole grounds for dismissal" and advised leaders to "avoid any actions regarding evaluation for dismissal that constitute harassment or intimidation."

When administrators have arrived at the decision to dismiss a teacher, Rebore (2012) emphasized a thoughtful and thorough process, including extensive documentation and consultation with the school's attorney to ensure the reasons are defensible. The author offered a familiar list of valid reasons for termination:

> Physical or mental condition unfitting him or her to instruct or associate with children; immoral conduct; insubordination, inefficiency, or incompetence in the line of duty; willful or persistent violation of, or failure to obey, the state laws pertaining to schools; willful or persistent violation of the published policies and procedures of the school board; excessive or unreasonable absence from work; a conviction of a felony or a crime involving moral turpitude. (p. 131)

As Associate Superintendent Lindaman pushes, Principal O'Donnell faces a real-world opportunity to sort through the law, her philosophy, protocol, and the "dance of the lemons."

THE TRANSCRIPT

Associate Superintendent:	Hi Emily. How are you doing?
Principal:	Hi Dr. Lindaman, Good to see you again.
Associate Superintendent:	Hi . . . good. Well, I'm gonna cut right to the chase here. Last week, once again, the three teachers that you and I've been talking about all along—John, Sue, Gary—um . . . raised all kinds

of havoc in my office. They are questioning policies, they're questioning all kinds of things and they're . . . the climate that they create in the building is not good. And here's what I'm thinking. I'm thinking they need to go. I think it's time, and so I guess what I'm gonna ask you to do is to get them out. And I think this is the last year for them. I think it's, I think it's time. And so, you know we have the April 15th deadline, so I guess I need to know what you're thinking, because in my mind, they've gotta go.

Principal: Well, I've only, I've only been here a couple months and I really . . . obviously, I've heard some things about, ah, you know, what their behavior is and I know they've come to see you a couple of times. Ah, I would like a chance to get to know them first and kind of see what their strengths are and ah, their weaknesses and then, um, and maybe see if I can, you know, change the culture or something that I'm gonna do this year, ah, makes them more of a community in our building. Uh, obviously I want to listen to them and see their side, but ah, I guess just see what . . . see what the real issues are . . .

Associate Superintendent: Right. Well, and I guess what I'd want you to understand is it's been . . . it's not just this year. It has been historically. You know, these are, two of them are veteran teachers, one of them is fairly new, about five years I think she's got five . . . six years. But, I think, I mean, I think if you look at everything that they've done over time, it's been a long time. And I think that they've worn out their welcome. I think it's about time that they go and I'm not sure that they would deserve . . . and I appreciate what you're thinking, but I'm thinking . . . they need to go. They need to go now.

Principal: Hmm. It's just really hard for me to dive into something like that when I'm not even really familiar with their teaching style, when I'm not familiar with, ah, with all of their history. I haven't been around long enough. Um, it's just, it's really hard for me to make judgments on people that I don't even really know right now. Um, obviously you have a longer history with them, but I'd still like to give them an opportunity to kind of prove themselves and see where they fit in my building and if we can find a place for them.

Associate Superintendent: Well, then what do you plan to do with them? I mean, how would you get to know them? I mean, what, what would you ... want to do with them to get to know them and to try to find out what the pattern is? What's your plan?

Principal: Um, well a lot of times, ah, you know, I want to start to try to build a relationship with them and maybe see where they're coming from. Um, a lot of times, um, teachers . . . I've taught with teachers that have been teaching a long time and they just, they feel that they're not heard and they don't always have the same opinions . . . .

Associate Superintendent: Oh, they're heard . . .

Principal: They don't always have the same, the same opinion, the same views, but sometimes we can work on that, you know, in professional leadership and um, I'd like to see my other teachers too and see their strengths and maybe we can do some things within the building and, um, you know, build some professional learning communities. Ah, we can structure our professional development around some of those concerns. Um, obviously, you know, if there are, if they're not a good fit, I'll be able to see that in a year or two, I would think, ah . . .

Associate Superintendent: Well, and the negativity I think of the two are . . . is the biggest issue. The negativity and the negative climate that they bring to the building. And I guess, you know I just, in my mind, like I said, I know you haven't had the history that I have with them for years and years, but um, that negativity is the thing that's probably gonna have to be addressed the most. And if it can't be under control, it's time for them to go.

Principal: Well, and I appreciate the fact that you're looking out for me because I think you're trying to defuse any future situations . . . Um, is there . . . I'm, I think all of them teach different subjects areas . . .

Associate Superintendent: Right.

Principal: Is there a different, um, maybe school that they could go to where ... if we split them up . . . I mean are they feeding off each other?

Associate Superintendent:	Well, and I guess that would be what you have to figure out. I don't know. I mean I do think that there is some sense of the fact that they feed off of each other. There's kind of a little bit of a mob mentality with the three of them . . . that they've certainly been heard . . . The squeaky wheel has been greased many times with them. The louder they get, the more attention they get and . . . so I'm just, I'm really concerned and it's not just for you, but it's for the whole building and I think, that's why I think, I mean I think this year has to be the end for them.

DISCUSSION AND REFLECTION QUESTIONS

1. Identify the key issue(s).
2. Identify the secondary issue(s).
3. Dr. Lindaman gets right at the point and says she thinks it is time for three teachers to "go." How should Principal O'Donnell respond? Should the fact that Emily is a new principal impact her response? Critique the response Principal O'Donnell gives at 40:47.
4. Dr. Lindaman leaves little question that she would like to have the three teachers gone. Are her reasons well-established? As human resources is her main area of responsibility, how much deference should Principal O'Donnell give to Dr. Lindaman's opinion?
5. Dr. Lindaman communicates directly and cuts right to the chase in her conversation with Emily. Principal O'Donnell seems less direct in her communication. Should she be more direct in expressing herself? Or is her approach practical, given that she is new and is talking with the associate superintendent?
6. At 42:35 Dr. Lindaman asks Principal O'Donnell to spell out her plan for getting to know the teachers in question. Evaluate Principal O'Donnell's response. Is this a plausible course of action? Is anything missing?
7. At 43:37 Principal O'Donnell suggests that within a year or two she should be able to identify the most important issues with the teachers. Dr. Lindaman identifies negativity and its impact on the school climate. Given that Dr. Lindaman has said the problems have been ongoing and are not limited to this year, is it appropriate for Principal O'Donnell to ask for a couple of years to work with them on these issues? On the other hand, is it appropriate for the associate superintendent to simply tell the new principal she thinks it is time for these teachers to go?

8. At 44:26 Principal O'Donnell asks if the teachers could be split up and sent to other schools. Is this a reasonable idea? Perhaps their negativity would be lessened if they were not allowed to "feed off each other," as Dr. Lindaman noted. On the other hand, if the teachers have had the negative impact she describes, is it ethical to send them to other buildings? Would Principal O'Donnell be engaged in the "dance of the lemons"?

9. Principal O'Donnell says she appreciates the associate superintendent looking out for her. Of course any administrator wants to trust their supervisor. It is certainly possible that the associate superintendent views the three teachers unfairly. Perhaps the teachers are raising legitimate issues that Dr. Lindaman simply doesn't want to hear. As a new leader, how can Principal O'Donnell:

- Demonstrate her competence to her supervisors;
- Respect the teachers in her building;
- Form her own opinions on the quality of the staff in her building;
- Act ethically and according to standards?

10. Is it possible that the associate superintendent is simply testing Principal O'Donnell? Perhaps she would like to see the three teachers go, but would be satisfied if their attitudes changed or they simply spent less time in her office complaining. Perhaps Principal O'Donnell's predecessor failed to provide instructional leadership and communication and the associate superintendent wants to see if Emily can do so. In what ways can we expect to be challenged as new leaders? To what challenges do you look forward? What challenges are less appealing to you?

11. The scenario ends with the associate superintendent indicating some flexibility in terms of the way Principal O'Donnell might deal with the three teachers immediately but sticks to her belief that this year should be "the end for them." Despite this belief, student performance or previous evaluations have not been mentioned. Does the negativity Dr. Lindaman describes sound like a sufficient reason for them to go?

12. What if at the end of the scenario Dr. Lindaman had said, "Emily, I appreciate your desire to get to know them and see if you can help them grow or at least stop the negativity. But *I* want them out of your building. Out of the district. At the end of the year, period. Can you do that?" How should she respond?

13. Would it be ethical for Principal O'Donnell to attempt to remove the three teachers by "driving them out" (i.e. assigning them the least desirable schedules, extra duties, and other things they would not like)? Would it be unethical if Principal O'Donnell told the three teachers directly that Dr. Lindaman wants them gone and that they must immediately work to improve their performance and change their attitudes or their contracts may be considered for termination?

14. Assume Principal O'Donnell determines that Dr. Lindaman is right and that her building would be better off without these three teachers. Should Principal O'Donnell employ whatever means necessary to see that they do not return? What should Principal O'Donnell do and not do?
15. Would it be reasonable to argue that perhaps these three teachers simply need a new start and fresh leadership that Principal O'Donnell may be able to provide?
16. Identify areas in which you believe the principal acted effectively.
17. Identify areas in which you believe the principal could have acted more effectively.

Balcony View

Generally speaking, how did the principal perform in this scenario? What would you have done differently?

Standards In Action

Which standards do you see as relevant in the scenario? Does the principal effectively meet them? Are there standards and/or criteria left unmet by the principal's actions?

Self Check

Picturing yourself in the principal's chair, describe your emotions. Does the case touch any of your biases or prior experiences?

Switch It Up

How might your thinking or approach change if the gender, social class, ethnicity, language, age, sexual orientation or other descriptors of the players involved were different?

Principal's Presence

In televised presidential debates, "looking presidential" is an important measure of a candidate's performance. The same is true for principals. Halpern and Lubar (2003, p. 3) define leadership presence as being more than "commanding attention" to include "the ability to connect authentically with the thoughts and feelings of others." Does the principal exert an effective "Principal's Presence?" Explain.

Principal's Priority

How *serious* is the situation?
How *soon* should the principal address this situation?
Should the principal inform/involve a *supervisor* on this issue?

In A Word

Capture the principal's performance in the scenario using one word.

Collaborate

Collaborate with a classmate or colleague to rewrite or alter the case with a different set of circumstances. Share your new case with other colleagues to ascertain how they would approach it.

Extension & Internship Experiences

- Discuss with an experienced principal, superintendent, or central office administrator the conditions under which they believe a teacher should be removed from the classroom. What are suggested decision points? What criteria make a teacher a candidate for counseling out versus a more overt termination process?
- What specific standards, laws, or district guidelines exist to help principals in your district or state determine when a teacher can and should be "counseled out" or terminated?
- Interview an experienced principal or central office administrator about "counseling" teachers out versus the ethics of "driving" a teacher out.

REFERENCES AND RESOURCES

Blase, J. (2009). School administrator mistreatment of teachers. *International Handbook of Research on Teachers and Teaching: Springer International Handbooks of Education, 21*(5), 433–448. doi: 10.1007/978-0-387-73317-3_28

Blase, J., & Blase, J. (2002). The dark side of leadership: Teacher perspectives of principal mistreatment. *Education Administration Quarterly, 38*(5), 671–727.

Blase, J., & Blase, J. (2003). *Breaking the silence: Overcoming the problem of principal mistreatment of teachers.* Thousand Oaks, CA: Corwin Press.

Blase, J., & Blase, J. (2003). The phenomenology of principal mistreatment: Teachers' perspectives. *Journal of Educational Administration, 41*(4), 367–422.

Blase, J., Blase, J., & Du, F. (2008). The mistreated teacher: A national study. *Journal of Educational Administration, 46*(3), 263–301.

Futernick, K. (2010). Incompetent teachers or dysfunctional systems? *Phi Delta Kappan, 92*(2), 59–64.

Henning, J. E., Kohler, F. W., Robinson, V. L., & Wilson, B. (2009). *Improving teacher quality: Using the teacher work sample to make evidence-based decisions.* Lanham, MD: Rowman and Littlefield.

Jazzar, M., & Algozzine, B. (2007). *Keys to 21st century educational leadership.* Upper Saddle River, NJ: Pearson.

Nolan, J. F., & Hoover, L. A. (2008). *Teacher supervision and evaluation: Theory into practice.* Hoboken, NJ: John Wiley & Sons.

Rebore, R. W. (2012). *The essentials of human resources administration in education.* Upper Saddle River, NJ: Pearson.

Schmoker, M. (2004). Tipping point: From freckles reform to substantive instructional improvement. *Phi Delta Kappan, 85*(6), 424–432. Retrieved from EBSCO*host*.

Thomas, E., & Wingert, P. (2010, March). Why we can't get rid of failing teachers. *Newsweek*, 24. Retrieved from http://www.newsweek.com

Webb, L. D., & Norton, M. S. (2009). *Human resources administration: Personnel issues and needs in education.* Upper Saddle River, NJ: Pearson.

Whitaker, T. (2002). *Dealing with difficult teachers.* (2nd ed.). Larchmont, NY: Eye on Education.

Whitaker, T. (2004). *What great teachers do differently: Fourteen things that matter most.* Larchmont, NY: Eye on Education.

Zepeda, S. J. (2007). *Instructional supervision: Applying tools and concepts.* (2nd ed.). Larchmont, NY: Eye on Education.

The Ruler and The Walkout (High School)

Jeremy is not a student who is usually in trouble at school. Thus, from the moment Jeremy shuffles into Principal Weires's office, she knows something is wrong. The sunken shoulders and defeated body language are a dead giveaway. As the upbeat Principal Weires prods Jeremy to tell her what has happened, Jeremy says he stood up for another student who was experiencing what is routine treatment in Mr. Jackson's class—being hit on the head with a ruler, little or no feedback on confusing assignments, and a teacher who is just "bad, bad, bad."

Jeremy explains that he and his fellow students have had enough poor treatment from Mr. Jackson. He says he came to the aid of a fellow student who, after not paying attention, was getting the familiar tap with the ruler. In confronting Mr. Jackson, Jeremy says he "told him where to stick the ruler." Jeremy claims that students have used Facebook to organize a walkout for tomorrow to show their feelings about Mr. Jackson.

This scenario reflects a familiar reality in schools—the complicated junction of personality, curriculum, rapport and classroom management, to name a few. While our students may be unfamiliar with the formal requirements of teacher evaluation, they certainly have their own measures of quality. Ravitch (2004, p. 162) famously labeled many students' school experience as an "Empire of Boredom." In Goodlad's classic, *A Place Called School* (1984, p. 9), he noted that many classrooms are places in which "boredom is a disease of epidemic proportion."

Sometimes boredom gives way to simple student resistance or lack of effort. Kohl's (1994) classic *I Won't Learn From You* is a must-read for educators searching for a path forward when resistant students show a "willful rejection of even the most compassionate and well-designed teaching" (p. 2). Books such as Cushman's (2003) *Fires in the Bathroom* and the subsequent *Fires in the Middle School Bathroom* (Cushman & Rogers, 2008) offered firsthand accounts of what many students seek from their teachers.

Many teachers can remember their first September when a veteran teacher cautioned, "Don't smile until after Thanksgiving." Regardless of whether we view the statement as sage advice or evidence of a dictatorial atmosphere that is likely to lead to an Empire of Boredom, everyone knows effective classroom management is essential to teaching success.

Whitaker and Whitaker (2006, p. 7) argued that "great teachers focus on expectations, other teachers focus on rules, and the least effective teachers focus on consequences of breaking the rules." In a related tone, Marzano and Marzano (2010, p. 160) cited research concluding, "that the quality of teacher-student relationships is the keystone for all other aspects of classroom management" and that " . . . teachers who had high-quality relationships with their students had 31 percent fewer discipline problems, rule violations, and related problems over a year's time than did teachers who did not have high quality relationships with their students."

With these issues on her mind, Principal Weires starts to listen to Jeremy's account of his (brief) day in algebra and what to do next.

THE TRANSCRIPT

Principal:	Jeremy! It is great to see you. How are you doing today? What's up? What's going on?
Student:	Mr. Jackson. He's a jerk.
Principal:	What happened?
Student:	You know how he walks around the room? And I know you know this cause all the kids know you know it. He walks around the room and if you're not paying attention or you didn't turn your homework in, or if you like, whisper something to somebody else, he's got that two foot ruler and he pops you on the head, you know. And I'm just sick and tired of it and so Andrew was over on the other side of the room and he was sitting there and he hit him and I stood up and I said, "Mr. Jackson, er, ah, Mr. Jackson, I said, if you have a problem with him why don't you just hit me with the ruler?" And I'm just not gonna take it anymore. I just . . . it's stupid and . . . tomorrow there'll be a walkout of his classroom. I've got him for sixth period. Every period, the students are walking out. We've got it all set up on Facebook and nobody's stopping it and we're just gonna walk out of the building. I mean, it's, we're tired of him . . . I mean just flat out tired of him.

Principal: So, have you talked to the teacher about the problem?

Student: No! He hits us with a ruler. Why would I talk to him? If I talk to him, he'll probably hit me harder.

Principal: Do you think he's hitting people, like to be mean, like hitting, hitting people or just like . . .

Student: He's a mean person. He's a bad teacher. He doesn't teach us anything. It's algebra class and he just gets on the board and writes $2x + 1 =$ I don't even know cause I don't learn anything in there.

Principal: How are you doing in that class?

Student: I don't know, he doesn't give us any grades.

Principal: Have you checked your grades online?

Student: Well, I ask him, he says he's working on my homework and he'll get it turned in and I'll have a grade soon. Well, it's like, I don't even know, midterm already and there's nothing posted. He probably doesn't even have his grades turned in.

Principal: So you sound really frustrated with the situation.

Student: Well, I'm not, I mean, he sent me out of the class because I told him where to stick the ruler and he didn't like it but the other kid, you know, he didn't do anything. All he was doing was just, he's not paying attention. Why would you pay attention? He's a terrible teacher. I don't know and so we're just gonna, just walk out. Every period, one through seven. Boom. We're all gonna walk out, walk out, walk out and we can . . . we all know we'll get in trouble by our parents but we don't care. We gotta make a point. This guy is bad . . .

Principal: Ok, Jeremy, let's go back to what happened in class today with you, because I suspect that very soon I'll be getting a write up . . .

Student: Oh, yeah.

Principal: Since you came, yeah.

Student: I'll be suspended.

Principal: Did he send you out or did you walk out? What happened there?

Student: No he said . . . he sent me out. I stood up and I told him what I told you about where to put the ruler and he said, "Get out. Go." And, ah . . . that's it.

Principal: Can I ask you what exactly did you say about where to put the ruler?

Student: Ah, I didn't say where to put the ruler. He knows where I want him to put the ruler.

Principal: You didn't say it?

Student: No, I didn't say that, but I said . . . he knows. And I don't ever get in trouble in his class. But I, he wasn't even directing the comment to me. It was Andrew. Andrew was sitting over there. He wasn't even doing anything wrong and . . . Whatever, I . . .

He's bad. I mean he's been bad. He's been here for twenty years. Go to hatemyteacher.com and boom! Mr. Jackson, right there. It's all up and down.

Principal: Yeah, well, I understand that you're frustrated with the whole situation. Um, is there anything else that I need to hear about what happened in class today from your side? Because I think until I talk to Mr. Jackson about what happened in class today, I can't make a decision about like you're suspended or anything like that and I hope it doesn't come to a situation like that . . .

Student: Oh, I'm gonna get suspended. He's gonna be pretty explicit in there, I'm pretty sure of it. And I'm gonna get in trouble with my parents, I know all that, but the whole point is . . . I guess it's about my behavior, but we haven't had any conversation about his behavior and what he does as a teacher. I don't know if . . . who evaluates him or who hired him or what, but, I mean, he's just bad. He's just bad, bad, bad.

Principal: When you say, "he's bad," alright, are you talking about the way he's teaching, are you having trouble with the way he's teaching and understanding the algebra?

Student: No, I mean . . .

Principal: Or is it other things?

Student: No, I honestly think it's the way he treats kids. When you walk around a classroom with a two foot ruler and tap kids, you know, on there . . . And then the days when people are like sleeping, he like, tosses a bean bag at you and hits you in the face so you wake up . . . He doesn't treat people right. And so, if . . . he may be a good teacher but he treats us so poorly that why would you want to learn from somebody that doesn't even care about you? It just doesn't make any sense.

Principal: So, it's like the personal relationship part that we're having trouble with? Not so much the what he's teaching or how he's teaching it?

Student: All seven . . . there's a lot of personal relationships, one through seven, cause everyone I talked to . . . he just . . . doesn't get along with anybody . . . just, you know . . . I don't know anyone who likes him. Maybe you do, I don't know.

Principal: Well, let's again, go back to what happened today, because we do need to sort that out. Alright, because, yeah, you know, I'll be making a call to your mom. She needs to know what happened and I'm sure you'll talk to her about it. Actually, we'll call her while you're sitting in here. We'll get her on the phone and get on the speaker. And I can talk to her about it, you can talk to her about it. We'll just kind of clear the air on today's situation. Um, again, I can't make any decisions about what's gonna happen as far as do you need to be suspended or do you need to be out of

	that classroom for a little while until I hear from Mr. Jackson . . .
	ok, to get more details.
Student:	Ok.
Principal:	But you're pretty sure he's not gonna be happy, huh?
Student:	No. He's not gonna be happy. And nor will my mother.
Principal:	Yeah. You gonna be able to handle that?
Student:	Oh, I made a mistake. I know I made a mistake and I'll live with
	that, but, you know, we'll see what happens.
Principal:	So let's, let's talk about how to get, like, to the root of this . . .

DISCUSSION AND REFLECTION QUESTIONS

1. Identify the key issue(s).
2. Identify the secondary issue(s).
3. Jeremy starts his conversation with Principal Weires by noting that Mr. Jackson is "a jerk" (45:26). Given that students are often upset when they're sent to the office for disciplinary reasons, what kind of response should the principal have to Jeremy referring to the teacher as a jerk? What if Jeremy had said Mr. Jackson was "a jackass?" "An asshole?" In other words, how should the principal go about gaining an understanding of what happened in the classroom without potentially piling more disciplinary sanctions on the student for the words he uses in answering her questions? Or should there be consequences for the words students use? If Mr. Jackson is later upset that Principal Weires allowed a student to call him "a jerk" without reprimanding the student, what should she say? Is Principal Weires on the right track letting the comment slide and trying to get Jeremy talking?
4. At 46:16 Jeremy first mentions a planned walkout of Mr. Jackson's classroom set for tomorrow. Evaluate Principal Weires's handling of the threat of the walkout. If it happens, the walkout would certainly cause a disruption. If you were in Principal Weires's shoes, how would you address the potential walkout?
5. At 46:42 Principal Weires asks Jeremy if Mr. Jackson is hitting students with the ruler to be mean or in some other context, but doesn't complete her question. Does Mr. Jackson's intent matter if he is indeed making contact with students with the ruler? Is he simply asking for trouble? Or is it possible that one of Mr. Jackson's mannerisms is to carry around a ruler and has occasionally touched students with it? Is it likely that Jeremy is exaggerating the story because he is in trouble?
6. Jeremy makes a number of complaints, from Mr. Jackson being mean, to not learning anything, to a lack of feedback on his grade, to Mr. Jackson being a bad teacher. Does Principal Weires effectively address each of

these issues? Are there some issues that she should not address with Jeremy because the main concern is that he has been kicked out of class? Or are all of the issues inherently related to his being sent to the office?

7. While a student walkout would certainly be disruptive, many students are sophisticated enough to object to what they see as ineffective teaching or inappropriate treatment from teachers. A walkout or protest organized online is not hard to envision. Many school mission statements include a desire to create engaged, participatory citizens. Given this and the role of peaceful protests have played in history, do the students have a right to express themselves in this way?

8. At 47:20 Jeremy says he told Mr. Jackson "where to stick the ruler." Does this raise the disciplinary stakes for Jeremy? Explain.

   In response to Principal Weires's question, Jeremy says most of the problems with Mr. Jackson are related to "the way he treats kids." Evaluate her response to Jeremy. Given his answer, how should she respond with Mr. Jackson? In a larger sense, how can a principal help teachers develop an effective rapport with students? Is this a principal's job?

9. Principal Weires notes that she cannot make any decisions on what will happen to Jeremy until she talks to Mr. Jackson about what happened. Describe the approach and specific questions you would ask Mr. Jackson. If in that conversation, Mr. Jackson says he expects respect from his students and that Jeremy was sent to the office for lack of respect and insubordination, how should Principal Weires respond?

10. Principal Weires indicates that she plans to call Jeremy's mother on the speaker phone with Jeremy present. Is this advisable? Explain. If she makes this call, should it be before or after she has talked with Mr. Jackson?

11. If in the phone conversation Jeremy's mother takes the position that Mr. Jackson caused the situation by "hitting" students with a ruler and that Jeremy should be commended for "standing up to that idiot," how should Principal Weires respond?

12. Given the emphasis that many schools place on character programs, respect, etc., is it possible that Jeremy's actions, while likely to bring some kind of disciplinary action, are warranted, given the way he says Mr. Jackson treats students? If Jeremy's accounts of Mr. Jackson tapping students with the ruler and tossing bean bags at sleeping students are true, is the teacher violating basic tenets of respect in the classroom?

13. Imagine Principal Weires making the following statement to Mr. Jackson: "In this day and age, if you're tapping kids on the head with a ruler, you're inviting one of them to react physically." Do you agree? Should she say this to Mr. Jackson? Imagine that Mr. Jackson responded, "I don't hit anyone. I tap them. And I'm walking around the room to keep

them engaged. You don't want me sitting behind the desk, do you?" How should Principal Weires respond?

14. Identify areas in which you believe the principal acted effectively.
15. Identify areas in which you believe the principal could have acted more effectively.

Balcony View

Generally speaking, how did the principal perform in this scenario? What would you have done differently?

Standards In Action

Which standards do you see as relevant in the scenario? Does the principal effectively meet them? Are there standards and/or criteria left unmet by the principal's actions?

Self Check

Picturing yourself in the principal's chair, describe your emotions. Does the case touch any of your biases or prior experiences?

Switch It Up

How might your thinking or approach change if the gender, social class, ethnicity, language, age, sexual orientation or other descriptors of the players involved were different?

Principal's Presence

In televised presidential debates, "looking presidential" is an important measure of a candidate's performance. The same is true for principals. Halpern and Lubar (2003, p. 3) define leadership presence as being more than "commanding attention" to include "the ability to connect authentically with the thoughts and feelings of others." Does the principal exert an effective "Principal's Presence?" Explain.

Principal's Priority

How *serious* is the situation?
How *soon* should the principal address this situation?
Should the principal inform/involve a *supervisor* on this issue?

In A Word

Capture the principal's performance in the scenario using one word.

Collaborate

Collaborate with a classmate or colleague to rewrite or alter the case with a different set of circumstances. Share your new case with other colleagues to ascertain how they would approach it.

Extension & Internship Experiences

- Identify a small number of teachers or leaders in your school or district who are known to have excellent rapport with students. Observe and interview them to learn about what they do to foster these relationships.
- Consider developing and administering a survey or focus group discussion with a group of students to learn about teacher qualities they find most important to support learning. Emphasize that you are not merely interested in popularity, but teaching practices that support their learning.
- Convene a group of teachers and/or students to explore the concept of teacher-student rapport and the difference between teachers being liked versus respected. What conclusions can be drawn from the conversation?

REFERENCES AND RESOURCES

Cushman, K. (2003). *Fires in the bathroom: Advice for teachers from high school students.* New York, NY: The New Press.

Cushman, K., & Rogers, R. (2008). *Fires in the middle school bathroom: Advice for teachers from middle schoolers.* New York, NY: The New Press.

Daniels, M. (2009). The three Fs of classroom management. *Journal of Scholarship and Practice, 6*(3), 18–24.

Goodlad, J. (1984). *A place called school: Prospects for the future.* New York: McGraw-Hill.

Kohl, H. (1994). *I won't learn from you and other thoughts on creative maladjustment.* New York, NY: The New Press.

Marzano, R. J., & Marzano, J. S. (2010). The key to classroom management. In K. Ryan & J. M. Cooper (Eds.), *Kaleidoscope: Contemporary and classic readings in education.* Belmont, CA: Wadsworth.

Ravitch, D. (2004). *The language police: How pressure groups restrict what students learn.* New York, NY: Vintage Books.

Whitaker, T., & Whitaker, B. (2006). *Study guide: What great teachers do differently: Fifteen things that matter most.* Larchmont, NY: Eye on Education.

Hot Seat #10

Pornography or Literature? (Middle School)

Mr. Jeff Dieken enjoys his reputation around town as a strong family man and a deacon in his church. "Deacon Dieken" stops by Principal Olsen's on a sunny Friday afternoon office to complain that several books assigned in his daughters' English classes are inappropriate.

From the moment he shakes Principal Olsen's hand, we sense an undercurrent of tension in their meeting. Mr. Dieken has brought with him books that are the sources of his objections, complete with highlighted passages and dog-eared pages. He begins making his case by reading aloud a steamy passage from one of the assigned books, *What's Eating Gilbert Grape?* As the conversation deepens, he also questions Principal Olsen about popular music being played during art class and whether she is blindly supporting her teachers, even to the point of promoting pornography.

Bolman and Deal (2010, p. 133) asserted that "most of the knotty issues in schools involve tough choices between competing values." Often those competing values relate to the way social issues, current events, popular culture, science, and religion permeate school walls. Perhaps the most famous case boiled over in Tennessee in 1925 in what is commonly known as the Scopes Monkey Trial, in which a high school teacher was accused of violating the state's ban on the teaching of evolution. A look at the day's top news stories demonstrates the interplay of these issues in schools is far from settled.

Other values-related controversies frequently involve literature and music. From what music should be played at the homecoming dance to controversies about whether language in *Huck Finn* should be edited and student access to books like *Heather Has Two Mommies*, principals routinely find themselves drawn into what some call the Culture War. Experienced principals know well the complexity of local definitions and expectations and parental concerns. They also know that issues that become major sources of controversy in one community may pass without attention in many others.

Martinson (1996) offered guidance for school administrators who find themselves responding to these issues. First, administrators should remember that those questioning these materials are often confident that they are doing the right thing on behalf of students. While administrators certainly want to make themselves and the schools look good, Martinson argued for a more productive focus on genuine communication that refrains from portraying the other side as an enemy.

The conversation between Principal Olsen and Deacon Dieken demonstrates this is sometimes easier said than done.

THE TRANSCRIPT

Principal:	Jeff, Angela Olson.
Dad:	Hi.
Principal:	Nice to meet you.
Dad:	Nice to meet you. Should we sit?
Principal:	If you'd like to sit, that would be great. What can I do for you today? Again, what can I do for you today?
Dad:	I have been . . . I have a daughter that's in eighth grade and a daughter that's in eleventh grade and they are doing some things in English class that are kind of bothering me. First let me tell you some things that's outstanding. Your middle school English teacher, Language Arts teacher really knows how to differentiate with students. You know, the kids that are a little lower? She helps them, the kind of average kids that are just going through the typical curriculum, and then the high end kids, they do get some, you know, higher stuff. Well, my daughter happens to be one of those that's, you know, a little higher. And ah, one of the books that um, that she, ah, is sharing with those higher kids . . . well, here's the book that they're reading in class. *Harry Potter and the Goblet of Fire* . . . Have you read any of these?
Principal:	I have not.
Dad:	Ok, well there's about thirty of them . . .
Principal:	Ok . . .
Dad:	. . . and they're all about this long and . . . you know, there's a lot of things like witches and warlocks which is not something that really . . . You know, I'm a deacon on the . . . "Deacon Dieken" on the Presbyterian service here in town and if the Presbytery heard about this, this would be a huge issue for them.

Principal:	Ok.
Dad:	So there's that. Well, she's a little more advanced so they wanted her to read this one, *What's Eating Gilbert Grape?* Have you seen that movie?
Principal:	I have not.
Dad:	Ok, well, it's a very, it's a great movie but in this, um, but there are some things . . . Let me just read you a couple things in this book. Now, she's in eighth grade . . .
Principal:	Ok.
Dad:	This is, I'll set this up for you. This is Gilbert talking with . . . um, this woman who he's having an affair with, um . . . "I'm dialing . . . " He's actually calling her husband while this is happening. I'm dialing, I hope this can wait 'til I'm done. She unzips my pants, kissing my tummy. She licks lower . . . I dialed wrong, I think, so I hung up and she giggles. I dial again, she pulls down my underwear, the phone's ringing . . . I say, ah, but there's no stopping her. She holds me in her hand and puts me in her mouth."
Principal:	Ok, so . . .
Dad:	Well, just a second . . . That's just one thing. I mean, then there's a part . . . I mean this book is full of masturbation and adultery and it's ah, there's another one here where . . . well, let me find it . . . I mean, I've got them marked . . . all over...
Principal:	Can I just ask you a couple of questions before you go on?
Dad:	Sure, sure.
Principal:	Um, so these were both eighth grade . . . am I understanding correctly that these were both books that your eighth grader was given to read as an assignment from the teacher?
Dad:	Yeah, but that's not it. My eleventh grader, um, and I know you're just middle school, but my eleventh grader was given these books. Now, um, this one is *The Awakening* by Kate Chopin . . . this one's about, ah, freedom, letting women, you know, giving them a way to escape life . . . And this is sex and adultery and . . . this, that's horrible. Now, my daughter, my older daughter, went about this the right way and said listen I'm not interested in reading that. And . . .
Principal:	Did she go to the teacher with that comment?
Dad:	Yes, absolutely, absolutely. And the teacher said "Ok, let me give you something else," which I think is probably right.
Principal:	Ok.
Dad:	Uh, but had this one, *The Bridges of Madison County*, now, have you read this one or seen the movie?
Principal:	I have seen the movie, yes.
Dad:	Ok, well, it's not the same. But this one's filled with, you know, the same thing. Ah, adultery, and you know, the photographer,

artistic, artsy-fartsy photographer comes to town and the wife is enamored with him . . . and eventually, you know, they end up having sex and, you know, it doesn't work. So, again, she read this book. She read the first book, wasn't, didn't really like it, said that I shouldn't be reading that, so she gave her this book and then she asked for a different one and they gave her, ah, *The Handmaid's Tale*, which I don't have cause she's still reading it but, would you like me to read you some things out of that one?

Principal: No, I think I have enough information from what you have gathered and what you have brought to me.

Dad: Oh, one other thing though, my eighth grader in art class, um, now I know you have an electronic policy, the school's, you know, no cell phones and iPods only in art class because it helps them be more creative and whatnot and I'm ok with that that. Well, the art teacher allows kids to bring in their iPods and she's got a fancy CD player that plays iPods. Well, some of the music that they're playing is a little over the top. For example, are you familiar with Soulja Boy?

Principal: I'm not. Can you just . . .

Dad: Ok, well there's this song called "Superman that Ass" or something like that . . .

Principal: Can I ask you, are these songs being played out loud or are these songs being played out loud or on the iPods?

Dad: Oh no, out loud! Yeah, cause they, it's like there's a dock and they plug it in and so my eighth grader is like, I don't know, they wanted to use that song for the talent show and I didn't really know. I can't understand what they're talking about but my eleventh grader, at dinner, we're sitting down and she's talking about Soulja Boy "Superman That Ass" or something like that and my eleventh grader says "What?!" And she explains what "Superman That Ass" is. Are you . . . Should I tell you . . . it has to do with ejaculation and masturbation and she . . .

Principal: No, I don't need any more information . . . I think I have the information that I need. Have you as a parent gone in to these teachers and expressed your concern and your frustration and your, ah, lack of wanting your children to read this type of literature?

Dad: Absolutely!

Principal: Have you gotten any, what types of responses have you received from the teachers?

Dad: They said we differentiate and we offer different books. But every book that they offer is something that . . .

Principal: Did you get any, um, curriculum-type, standard and benchmark reasoning for why they're selecting the books that . . . did you ask for any of that type of information?

Dad:	No, I didn't because I just didn't think that adultery and pornography was in any sort of benchmark. I mean, I figured that you know . . .
Principal:	Well, and I don't think it is.
Dad:	You know, it might be at the school on the other side of the tracks but this school . . .
Principal:	I guess my point is did you, did you express to them the exact concern you have with the type of material that they are having your daughters read?
Dad:	I asked, "Are you giving my kids books that have pornography in them" and they said "That's literature. These are books by authors who are renown around the world and have been for a long time." And I said again, "Are you giving my kids books about pornography?" And neither of them would answer. You know, but my beef is more with the eighth grade teacher . . .
Principal:	That's a situation that I will, that I will need to look into. I will take the concerns, I will take the titles of the book . . .
Dad:	How old are eighth grade students typically?
Principal:	Thirteen, fourteen, fifteen.
Dad:	Ok, so a thirteen year old learning about boys masturbating and . . . and I mean . . .
Principal:	I understand your concern as a parent. I do. I understand your concern as a parent.
Dad:	But you're not . . . do you have kids? Because, I mean, I'm sitting here thinking that you understand it, but you should be irate! You should be irate.
Principal:	I do have children. Yes. I do have children. I just, I need you to understand that I am going to support my teachers as well, but I need to go find out the . . .
Dad:	Oh! Wait, wait, wait. You're going to support your teachers while . . .
Principal:	You need to let me finish, please.
Dad:	You're gonna support your teachers of promoting pornography to my eighth grade . . .
Principal:	Well, until I find . . . No . . . I did not say I would support everything, I just need to go find out . . .
Dad:	You know what? I'm just thinking that Deacon Dieken . . . should go to the church now and open up a whole firestorm of stuff that's going on.
Principal:	Well, and when I said that, I meant that I need to go to them and find out the information from them . . .
Dad:	It's easy to back away . . . typically we say things that we mean first off. You don't . . . you're trying to come back now and say that, you know, I understand . . .

DISCUSSION AND REFLECTION QUESTIONS

1. Identify the key issue(s).
2. Identify the secondary issue(s).
3. Mr. Dieken raises a concern about some of the reading materials that his daughters are being asked to read in English classes. He asks Principal Olsen if she has read a number of them. She has not. Is it the principal's responsibility to read or be familiar with instructional materials that may become controversial? Or is that unrealistic?
4. At 53:22 Mr. Dieken reads a passage from *What's Eating Gilbert Grape?* Describe any *personal* feelings you have about the book or the passage. Do you feel the book is appropriate for the eighth graders? Do you feel qualified to make that judgment without reading the entire book? Is this decision better made by others, such as the English department, school board, or a committee?
5. Describe your emotions as Mr. Dieken reads the passage from *What's Eating Gilbert Grape?* How would you respond? Evaluate Principal Olsen's response.
6. Some would say that Mr. Dieken is working hard to exert masculine power in this scenario from the moment he holds Principal Olsen's hand for an unusually long length of time. Do you agree? Given the content of the passage he reads, do you believe he is trying to intimidate Principal Olsen? Is he trying to capitalize on sexual tension that may be present in their interaction? Do you believe Mr. Dieken would choose to read the same passage to a male principal? Is this a situation in which Principal Olsen should be prepared to communicate with a colleague or secretary through a secret signal that she may need assistance or be in a vulnerable position?
7. At 54:18 Mr. Dieken continues with some objections to materials his eleventh grade daughter was given to read, though he acknowledges that Principal Olsen is only in charge of middle school. Should she try to redirect his attention to only the middle school issues or is it better to allow him to express all of his concerns? Explain.
8. At 55:46 Mr. Dieken shifts his attention to some of the music being played in the art room via students' iPods and the teacher's CD player. Evaluate Principal Olsen's questioning and response to this concern. After Mr. Dieken raises the music issue, the conversation returns to the reading materials. Should the principal continue to explore the concern over the music?
9. When Principal Olsen tries to make a connection between the curriculum and teachers' choices of reading material, Mr. Dieken says he didn't think "adultery and pornography were in any sort of benchmark." He then references that perhaps these materials are acceptable at other schools.

   On the surface, many schools and communities appear to be quite similar. Experienced educators, however, know that culture, climate and context account for some major differences. It is likely the issue Mr. Dieken is raising might never surface in a nearby school. How can a principal gain a sense of local opinions on issues like this and anticipate potential reactions?

10. After establishing that Mr. Dieken raised his concerns with the teachers, Principal Olsen says she will discuss the issue and the books with the teacher and that she understands his concerns (58:10). At 58:41 she indicates that she will support her teachers, to which Mr. Dieken objects further.

    Evaluate this exchange and the principal's message. Teachers repeatedly identify principal support as being very important, yet Mr. Dieken seems intent on using this against the principal here. Ultimately he threatens to create a stir in the community through a church group. How would you have handled this exchange?

    At this point, the conversation seems more contentious than a few minutes prior. How should Principal Olsen attempt to bring closure to the conversation? What should happen next? Should Principal Olsen be concerned that Mr. Dieken will leave the meeting telling people that the principal said the books were fine and that she intended to support the teachers' efforts to teach what he believes to be inappropriate? On the other hand, should the principal be concerned that the teachers may think she failed to support their curricular and instructional decisions firmly enough when questioned?

11. One district attracted a considerable amount of media attention after a district administrator pulled *What's Eating Gilbert Grape?* from the library shelves and English curriculum after a parent objected to the book's content. The administrator acknowledged having not read the book. Was this decision appropriate?

12. From *The Ed Sullivan Show*'s restrictions on The Beatles, The Rolling Stones, and The Doors, controversies over song lyrics are nothing new. Yet digital technology and instant downloads make a principal's job more complicated. Numerous online sources such as urbandictionary.com suggest that the lyrics in "Crank That" (Soulja Boy Tell 'Em, 2007) are misogynistic with references to masturbation, sex, etc. Though the artist argued these interpretations were not what he intended, such controversies leave school administrators to navigate the complicated intersection of intent, local context, free speech, and community standards.

    Some have argued that the use of music aids in creativity, but does Mr. Dieken have a legitimate concern over the songs being played in art class? Practically speaking, how can a principal stay current on songs that might be objectionable in a school setting?

13. Is this a situation in which a principal should have another person present during the conversation? Explain.

14. Identify areas in which you believe the principal acted effectively.

15. Identify areas in which you believe the principal could have acted more effectively.

Balcony View

Generally speaking, how did the principal perform in this scenario? What would you have done differently?

Standards In Action

Which standards do you see as relevant in the scenario? Does the principal effectively meet them? Are there standards and/or criteria left unmet by the principal's actions?

Self Check

Picturing yourself in the principal's chair, describe your emotions. Does the case touch any of your biases or prior experiences?

Switch It Up

How might your thinking or approach change if the gender, social class, ethnicity, language, age, sexual orientation or other descriptors of the players involved were different?

Principal's Presence

In televised presidential debates, "looking presidential" is an important measure of a candidate's performance. The same is true for principals. Halpern and Lubar (2003, p. 3) define leadership presence as being more than "commanding attention" to include "the ability to connect authentically with the thoughts and feelings of others." Does the principal exert an effective "Principal's Presence?" Explain.

Principal's Priority

How *serious* is the situation?
How *soon* should the principal address this situation?
Should the principal inform/involve a *supervisor* on this issue?

In A Word

Capture the principal's performance in the scenario using one word.

Collaborate

Collaborate with a classmate or colleague to rewrite or alter the case with a different set of circumstances. Share your new case with other colleagues to ascertain how they would approach it.

Extension & Internship Experiences

- Examine your school or district policy on challenges to instructional materials. Is it well-communicated to parents and the community? Speak with a secretary, teacher, or administrator with a long history in the school or district to determine how frequently, if ever, objections have been raised and how/if they were resolved.
- Access the American Library Association's website (www.ala.org) and peruse the information on banned and challenged books, noting if your school or district uses any of the books identified.
- Interview an experienced administrator about how s/he stays informed and handles potentially controversial or inappropriate lyrics or music in a school setting. Does the school have an official policy for acceptable song lyrics for dances and what may be played at school? Do administrators use established criteria to determine acceptability or make determinations on a case by case basis?
- Interview a female administrator to explore her thoughts on gender and the principalship. Can she recount incidences of harassment, discrimination, or interactions in which male colleagues, parents, or others seemed intent on intimidation or bullying related to gender? Does she identify with the oft-heard notion that a woman must be twice as good as a man to be seen as effective?

REFERENCES AND READING

Ah Nee-Benham, M. K. P., & Cooper, J. E. (1998). *Let my spirit soar: Narratives of diverse women in educational leadership*. Thousand Oaks, CA: Corwin Press.

Atwood, M. (1986). *The handmaid's tale*. Boston, MA: Houghton-Mifflin.

Blume, J. (1999, October 22). Is Harry Potter evil? *New York Times*, p. A27.

Bolman, L. G., & Deal, T. E. (2010). *Reframing the path to school leadership: A guide for teachers and principals*. (2nd ed.). Thousand Oaks, CA: Corwin Press.

Chopin, K. (2011). *The awakening*. London, England: Random House UK Ltd.

Cobb, M. D., & Boettcher III, W. A. (2007). Ambivalent sexism and misogynistic rap music: Does exposure to Eminem increase sexism? *Journal of Applied Psychology*, *37*(12), 3025–3042.

DeMitchell, T. A., & Carney, J. J. (2005). Harry Potter and the public school library. *Phi Delta Kappan*, *87*(2), 159–165. Retrieved from EBSCO*host*.

Gause, C. P. (2005). Navigating the stormy seas: Critical perspectives on the intersection of popular culture and educational leader-"Ship." *Journal of School Leadership, 15*(3), 333–342.

Goldwasser, M. M. (1997). Censorship: How it happened to me in southwest Virginia: It could happen to you too. *The English Journal, 86*(2), 34–42.

Grogan, M. & Shakeshaft, C. (2011). *Women and educational leadership.* San Francisco, CA: Jossey-Bass.

Hedges, P. (2005). *What's eating Gilbert Grape?.* New York, NY: Simon & Schuster Paperbacks.

Hess, D. E. (2009). *Controversy in the classroom: The democratic power of discussion.* New York, NY: Routledge.

Hicks, A. T. (1996). *Speak softly and carry your own gym key: A female high school principal's guide to survival.* Thousand Oaks, CA: Corwin Press.

Hill, M. S., & Ragland, J. C. (1995). *Women as educational leaders: Opening windows, pushing ceilings.* Thousand Oaks, CA: Corwin Press.

Knoboch-Westerwick, S., Musto, P., & Shaw, K. (2009). Rebellion in the top music charts: Defiant messages in rap/hip hop and rock music 1993 and 2003. *Journal of Media Psychology, 20*(1), 15–23.

Martinson, D. L. (1996). Confront censorship crusades with genuine school-community relations. *Journal of Educational Relations,* 12. Retrieved from EBSCO*host.*

Newman, L., & Souza, D. (2009). *Heather has two mommies.* Los Angeles, CA: Alyson Wonderland.

Petress, K. (2005). The role of censorship in school. *Journal of Instructional Psychology, 32*(3), 248–252.

Ravitch, D. (2004). *The language police: How pressure groups restrict what students learn.* New York, NY: Vintage Books.

Reichman, H. (2001). *Censorship and selection: Issues and answers for schools.* Chicago, IL: American Library Association.

Rowell, C. (1986). Allowing parents to screen textbooks would lead to anarchy in the schools. *Chronicle of Higher Education, 33*(26), 34.

Rowling, J. K. (2000). Harry Potter and the goblet of fire. New York, NY: Arthur A. Levine Books.

Shakeshaft, C., Nowell, I., & Perry, A. (2007). *Gender and supervision. In the Jossey-Bass Reader on Educational Leadership.* (2nd ed.). (339-348). San Francisco, CA: Jossey-Bass.

Soulja Boy Tell 'Em. (Performer). (2007). Crank that (Soulja Boy). On *souljaboytellem. com* [CD]. Santa Monica, CA: Interscope.

Twain, M. (1990). *Adventures of Huckleberry Finn.* New York, NY: Chelsea House.

Walker, J. M. (2010). It takes at least two to tangle. *Journal of Cases in Educational Leadership, 13*(4), 22–43. doi: 10.1177/1555458910381464

Waller, R. J. (1992). *The bridges of Madison County.* New York, NY: Warner Books.

Hot Seat #11

Nobody's Boy (High School)

In this scenario, Willie, a star African American football player and talented student arrives in the office complaining that a teacher called him "boy." As he protests about the racial slur, Willie shares his frustration with the teacher's personality and the way he interacts with kids. When Principal Hawkins learns that Willie has already called his mom and she is likely on her way to school, she's faced with a delicate situation rife with socially-constructed assumptions about race, gender, language, and power and little time to decide her next step.

Some educators have lamented that, even in an increasingly diverse nation, being white in parts of the United States means never having to think about race/ethnicity and the privilege it affords. While some have never actively considered the impact of race, others such as Eric Holder, the first African American Attorney General of the United States, have suggested that America is a "nation of cowards" that avoids serious dialog about race.

In her classic essay *White Privilege: Unpacking the Invisible Knapsack*, McIntosh (1990) theorized that white people are taught not to recognize white privilege. Howard (2006, p. 79) suggested that "too often, the legacy of privilege and the legacy of ignorance have prevented us from seeing and hearing one another." Delpit (1995) built on the age-old adage of walking in another's shoes in order to fully realize the promise of effective communication and education across all groups.

When we teach across the boundaries of race, class and gender—indeed when we teach at all—we must recognize and overcome the power differential, the stereotypes and the other barriers which prevent us from seeing each other. (p. 134)

Consider how effectively Principal Hawkins handles these issues on a
moment's notice.

THE TRANSCRIPT

Principal:	Hi. How are you, Willie?
Student:	Not good.
Principal:	You're not good?
Student:	Not good at all.
Principal:	Well come on in and let's talk about this. Have a seat. What's going on? You've got a big game coming up. What's going on here?
Student:	No, I'm sitting in class and we're working on something. And I can't remember if I was talking or what was going on and then I look over at the teacher and he's sitting there and he said something along the lines of "Boy, you better shut up" or "Boy . . ." something or something along those lines and I don't play that stuff.
Principal:	Ok, can you tell me what class this was?
Student:	It was in math class.
Principal:	Math class. And who's your teacher again?
Student:	Mr., ah, Falubell.
Principal:	Mr. Falubell, ok, ok. And, so what were you doing prior to this that . . . were you talking to someone . . .?
Student:	We were just sitting there talking, we were just sitting there talking.
Principal:	You were talking with who?
Student:	With Santrise.
Principal:	Ok. And you were just . . . was he doing instruction on the board or . . .
Student:	don't know what he was doing. It doesn't matter what he was doing! He can't call me a boy! That's like calling me a nigger. There ain't no difference.
Principal:	Well, I think we . . .
Student:	So, we're all focused on what I was doing. He's the one that's in the wrong, not me! He . . . yeah, I shouldn't have been talking but he can't call me that.
Principal:	Ok, so . . .
Student:	He's lucky I didn't knock his ass out.
Principal:	Ok, now first of all, you need to relax for a second, ok? We're just gonna talk in a normal tone of voice and we're gonna get to the bottom of this. Ok? We'll figure out a solution . . .
Student:	What are you gonna do?
Principal:	We're gonna get to the bottom of it and we'll find a solution, but first you have to understand that when you're sitting in a

classroom and when the teacher is up in front of the class giving instruction, your job as a student is to be there, cause your job is to learn, right? If you have a question, you raise your hand and you ask the teacher the question. You don't ask who's sitting next to you, who's sitting behind you. Cause if your conversation . . .

Student: What does that have to do with him calling me a boy? Tell me . . . Make the connection for me.

Principal: The problem first of all is that you were not behaving in the way that you should have. Now, as far as what he called you or what he said, that's a situation that we'll talk with him about that . . .

Student: I was talking and there was nobody . . . everybody talks in that class all the time. So my talking is no different than anything else going on in there.

Principal: So when he's up in front giving instruction, everybody in the class is just randomly . . .

Student: Have you observed him lately?

Principal: When I observed him I did not see that behavior in the class.

Student: Then you were in the wrong class.

Principal: Cause when I was observing, everybody was paying attention, they were doing their math problems and he actually gave a very good, ah, instruction that day. He gave a good lesson. So, I think that . . .

Student: That day. Ok.

Principal: Well, the days that I've been in there. And granted, I'm not in there every single day like you are, but I do stop in and check on my teachers and see the different things and interactions that are going on in the classroom. How is your relationship with him outside of the math?

Student: Not his boy.

Principal: Ok, so do you have conversations with him . . .

Student: I'm a student in that class just like everybody else. Not his boy.

Principal: Have you had . . . have you had conflict with him in the past?

Student: Not that I can recall.

Principal: Ok, so today's just kind of an isolated incident. Otherwise, he's been friendly to you,

Student: Isolated racist incident, yeah.

Principal: Has he been friendly to you? Do you feel as if, up to this point . . .

Student: He talks crazy to everybody in there, so I don't . . .

Principal: Do you think that he . . . he's treated you equally except for this . . .

Student: I think, yeah, he treats me like everybody else. He talks to me crazy like he talks to everybody else. It's not, that's . . . that's his personality.

Principal: Ok, and what's your current grade in his class?

Student:	An A.
Principal:	Oh, good. So obviously he's a good teacher and . . .
Student:	Obviously I'm a good student.
Principal:	And you are a good student, yeah, just like you're a good football player, too. Right?
Student:	So, again, what does this have to do with him calling me a boy and what are you gonna do about it? Cause I can tell you what. When I go home and get my mom involved—matter of fact, I ain't even gonna wait for that. When I called her, and matter of fact, she's probably already on her way up here, cause when I called . . .
Principal:	You called your mom on your way up here?
Student:	Heck yeah.
Principal:	That's ok, we'll have your mom come in and I think we'll also go get him . . .
Student:	Oh and when she comes in, you better make sure there's a security guard between him and her cause I'm telling you, she ain't gonna play that either.
Principal:	Yeah, and you know when I look in my files here, it looks like he has a prep period next period. And so I think what we'll do is we'll keep you in here with me and we'll continue having a conversation and if your mom comes, she can come have a seat. And then the four of us will sit down we'll discuss the situation . . .
Student:	And what are you gonna do about him calling me a boy?
Principal:	First of all, we need to find out how this all happened. You know, I need to hear that yes, you know, maybe you misunderstood what he was saying . . . Maybe if you were talking . . .
Student:	Nah, boy is boy. You know, I'm not a toy, so I guess it could've been that, but boy is boy.
Principal:	Well sometimes when you're having a conversation with somebody else, you might have caught the tail end of his conversation and then . . .
Student:	Boy, you need to quit talking, I think is pretty . . . .yeah.
Principal:	So, and I don't think that he meant it to be anything racial.
Student:	What do you think he meant it as, then?
Principal:	I think sometimes teachers would say, like I might say, ah, you know if you would come in and I'd see that you had a good game last night I'd say, "Hey, you know, way to go last night," or "Hey, boy, you had a great game," or "Hey, guy," or, ah, that's just conversation . . .
Student:	And I'd make it real clear to you that I wasn't your boy, either.
Principal:	And I'm not saying that you are my boy.
Student:	Ok.

DISCUSSION AND REFLECTION QUESTIONS

1. Identify the key issue(s).
2. Identify the secondary issue(s).
3. Does Principal Hawkins establish whether Mr. Falubell sent Willie out of the classroom or whether Willie left on his own? Does it matter? Explain.
4. Evaluate Principal Hawkins' response to Willie's assertion (1:00:23) that Mr. Falubell is lucky he "didn't knock his ass out." Would you respond in the same way? Should/could she interpret Willie's comment as a threat that should be addressed?
5. At 1:00:31 Principal Hawkins says she intends to get to the bottom of the situation in "a normal tone of voice" followed by telling Willie that his job as a student is to pay attention, raise his hand, etc. Evaluate.
6. Willie is unmoved by Principal Hawkins' review of his responsibilities as a student. Evaluate her assertion (1:00:40) that the first problem is that he was misbehaving. How should she respond to Willie's apparent belief that he was singled out because of his race, when students talking is common in the classroom?
7. It may not be surprising that Willie asked Principal Hawkins if she has seen what goes on in Mr. Falubell's classroom, given his claim that students routinely talk during instruction, etc. Evaluate her response to his question about whether she has observed in the classroom. Is it appropriate for Principal Hawkins to discuss what she observed or her judgment of the quality of instruction? Does this part of the conversation merely confuse the issue? Or is it a relevant part of the discussion because she is trying to establish the level of truth in Willie's claim that random student talking is common in Mr. Falubell's classroom?
8. Evaluate Principal Hawkins' decision to bring Mr. Falubell in to the office for a conversation next period, possibly with Willie, his mother, and the principal. Would you proceed the same way? Would you be concerned about Willie's suggestion of having a security guard present?
9. If you would not have this meeting next period, describe how you would proceed. Describe the conversation and questions you would have with Mr. Falubell.
10. As Willie continues to press Principal Hawkins to tell him what she plans to do about Mr. Falubell's alleged use of the word "boy," she suggests that Willie may have taken it out of context—an argument Willie quickly dismisses. Is it reasonable for a white person to tell a person of color that the statement in question was taken out of context? Explain.
11. At 1:02:31 Principal Hawkins asks Willie about his grade in the class. She concludes that Mr. Falubell must be a good teacher since Willie has

an A. Willie counters that he is a good student. What does it appear that Principal Hawkins is trying to do at this point in the conversation? Is it successful? Advisable? How would you proceed at this point?

12. At 1:03:43 Principal Hawkins suggests that she does not believe Mr. Falubell intended his statement to "be anything racial." Is this a good example of the principal supporting and defending the teacher? Or is it a case of the principal automatically defending the teacher before collecting enough information?

13. How should Principal Hawkins respond if she determines that the situation points to a lack of cultural competency or prejudice on the part of Mr. Falubell and/or others?

14. Can Principal Hawkins, as a white woman, adequately understand the Willie's position as a minority? How do Willie's and the principal's racial identities complicate the exchange?

15. Overall, how well does Principal Hawkins handle the situation with Willie? Does it appear that she is most focused on convincing Willie that there was no racist intent on the part of Mr. Falubell? If so, should she be more neutral?

16. Identify areas in which you believe the principal acted effectively.

17. Identify areas in which you believe the principal could have acted more effectively.

Balcony View

Generally speaking, how did the principal perform in this scenario? What would you have done differently?

Standards In Action

Which standards do you see as relevant in the scenario? Does the principal effectively meet them? Are there standards and/or criteria left unmet by the principal's actions?

Self Check

Picturing yourself in the principal's chair, describe your emotions. Does the case touch any of your biases or prior experiences?

Switch It Up

How might your thinking or approach change if the gender, social class, ethnicity, language, age, sexual orientation or other descriptors of the players involved were different?

Principal's Presence

In televised presidential debates, "looking presidential" is an important measure of a candidate's performance. The same is true for principals. Halpern and Lubar (2003, p. 3) define leadership presence as being more than "commanding attention" to include "the ability to connect authentically with the thoughts and feelings of others." Does the principal exert an effective "Principal's Presence?" Explain.

Principal's Priority

How *serious* is the situation?
How *soon* should the principal address this situation?
Should the principal inform/involve a *supervisor* on this issue?

In A Word

Capture the principal's performance in the scenario using one word.

Collaborate

Collaborate with a classmate or colleague to rewrite or alter the case with a different set of circumstances. Share your new case with other colleagues to ascertain how they would approach it.

Extension & Internship Experiences

- The issue of *intent* often surfaces in cases involving perceived harassment. Often, those accused of making offending statements say "I didn't mean anything by it." Many leaders advise that the person making the statement is not the one who gets to determine whether it is offensive. The one who hears it does. Ask the official responsible for initial harassment investigations in your school or district to review procedures and share questioning techniques with you.
- Examine relevant demographic changes in your school or district over the past five, ten, or twenty years. What, if any, changes have taken place? What, if any, professional development opportunities for staff have specifically addressed these changes? If not, investigate how the school or district might provide a relevant and effective experience.
- Hall and Hord (2011) suggest that examining issues that are present in school but seem forbidden for discussion is important for exploring school

culture and climate. Conduct an informal survey of students and/or teachers to identify issues they believe are rarely openly discussed.

• Consider developing a teachers' discussion/study group around McIntosh's *White Privilege* essay or similar resource.

REFERENCES AND RESOURCES

Barrett, D. (2009, February 19). Holder says Americans afraid to talk about race. *Boston Globe*. Retrieved from http://www.boston.com/news/nation/washington/articles/2009/ 02/19/holder_says_americans_afraid_to_talk_about_race/?page=full

Brown, D. F. (2004). Urban teachers' professed classroom management strategies. *Urban Education, 39*(3), 266–289. doi: 10.1177/0042085904263258

Delpit, L. (1995). *Other people's children: Cultural conflict in the classroom.* New York, NY: The New Press.

Hall, G. E., & Hord, S. M. (2011). *Implementing change: Patterns, principles, and potholes.* (3rd ed.). Boston, MA: Pearson.

Henderson, A. (2003) What's in a slur? *American Speech, 78*(1), 52–74.

Howard, G. R. (2006). *We can't teach what we don't know: White teachers, multiracial schools.* (2nd ed.). New York, NY: Teachers College Press.

Klotz, M. (2006). Culturally competent schools: Guidelines for secondary school principals. *Principal Leadership (Middle School Ed.), 6*(7), 11–14. Retrieved from Education Full Text database.

Marshall, C., & Oliva, M. (2010). *Leadership for social justice: Making revolutions in education.* (2nd ed.). Boston, MA: Allyn & Bacon.

McIntosh, P. (1990). White privilege: Unpacking the invisible knapsack. *Independent School, 49*(2), 31. Retrieved from EBSCO*host*.

McKenzie, K. B. (2009). Emotional abuse of students of color: The hidden inhumanity in our schools. *International Journal of Qualitative Studies in Education, 22*, 129–143.

Singleton, G. E., & Linton, C. (2006). *Courageous conversations about race: A field guide for achieving equity in schools.* Thousand Oaks, CA: Corwin Press.

Teel, K. M., & Obidah, J. E. (2008). *Building racial and cultural competence in the classroom: Strategies from urban educators.* New York, NY: Teachers College Press.

Hot Seat #12

Role Confusion (High School)

The principal in this scenario, Mr. Smock, faces a difficult dilemma with his superintendent. The overbearing, pushy superintendent, Dr. Horn, has a well-earned reputation for getting his way and a penchant for putting words in other people's mouths. Listening is an unfamiliar concept. On the morning after the high school volleyball team lost another match, the superintendent blows into Principal Smock's office complaining about the team and its coach. Dr. Horn has concluded that the team's performance, along with his daughter Megan's lack of playing time, warrant firing the coach. Principal Smock wades through a largely one-way conversation, hoping to steer his manic supervisor toward a reasonable course of action.

Whitaker (2003, p. 16) identified the principal as "the decisive element in the school." In the same vein, West and Darrington (2009) noted that, "although a district has many teams, the group that includes the principals and superintendent is arguably the most powerful . . . . These leaders intuitively understand the need for harmonious relationships to achieve goals that require working together" (p. 3). Principals fortunate enough to be a part of an effective leadership team can readily testify to the positive difference these working relationships make. Many school leaders benefit from being members of honest, efficient leadership teams.

However, such is not always the case. West and Darrington (2009, p. 5) also lamented the "disconnect when the superintendent expects collegial behavior in schools but does not cultivate a similar atmosphere within the leadership team." The authors noted that the example set by the superintendent invariably filters through to the principals and teachers, ultimately providing "either an exemplary role model to emulate or a dysfunctional example to deride" (p. 5).

As Dr. Horn vents his wish to get more playing time for his daughter or find a convenient way to fire the volleyball coach, Principal Smock wrangles with Dr. Horn's inability to separate his role as a father from that of superintendent. This gives Principal Smock a firsthand opportunity to experience the difficulty when familial loyalties and professional roles collide. Can he steer his boss toward professionalism and adherence to official district policy?

THE TRANSCRIPT

Superintendent:	Yeah, hey, nice job. Hey, when are you gonna deal with that situation with Marge?
Principal:	Ah, which one?
Superintendent:	That low cut, she's wearing that low crap. I told you, we've gotta be done with that . . . ah, I'm not here to talk about that anyway. What do you think about that volleyball last night?
Principal:	The kids are playing well.
Superintendent:	Well, yeah, but they lost again. I mean, that's three in a row in the fifth set . . . (phone rings) Excuse me. Jeez, sorry about that. Yeah, hello? No, I'm not gonna come and get you. I don't care if the damn car won't start. You get yourself here. You walk five blocks, it's no big deal. And you know I'm gonna check what you're wearing cause you looked like a whore the other day. Alright. Thanks. Yeah, love you too, Megan. Bye. Alright, so about the volleyball. We were talking about the volleyball, right? So, what do you think about that . . . all this losing we're doing? What's your opinion? You were there, standing there leaning up against the wall and the whole bit. So what do you think?
Principal:	I think, I know coach said some of the girls are coming off the flu and stuff like that . . .
Superintendent:	Yeah, I agree with that. I think it has a lot to do with the coach. I am in total agreement with that. You know, cause the girls are trying like you said . . . I mean they're out there, and they're trying, doing everything they can do, they're practicing hard. You know, they're working their spandex off is what I think's happening . . . and you know, then they're still losing. And that's really disheartening, don't you think?
Principal:	Well, it's tough. A tough conference this year, I mean everybody's . . . I know West has most of their people back . . . (phone rings)

Superintendent:	Ah, excuse me. Jeez. Sorry. Sorry. Yeah? I don't care. No, you can do it. Well, then call Shannon and get a ride. If you can't walk five blocks, my God, you're supposed to be an athlete and the whole bit. Alright. Yeah. See you honey. Alright, bye. Ok, sorry about that.
Principal:	You know, I've got some other things, if you need to go get your daughter . . . that's perfectly fine . . . .
Superintendent:	No, Jeez, that's fine no, she can do it. I mean, how are these kids gonna learn if I'm in here fighting for her all the time? I mean there's no way she's gonna learn, but anyway that's part of it, I think. You know, don't you think she ought to be playing more?
Principal:	Ah . . . I guess I haven't talked to Coach Johnson about it, you know, to see how everything's going . . .
Superintendent:	Ok, but you're gonna do that? Are you gonna talk to her about having my daughter play more? Because you know that'd make a huge difference. And you know, well, we talked about this last night . . . when we were complaining about the officials . . . remember you yelling at the officials? Oh my God, that was great . . .
Principal:	I thought that ball was in.
Superintendent:	It was in, you're absolutely right, I like that . . . that was great . . . that thing was in. Oh, man, but anyway, so you got any coffee? Hey Marge, get me some coffee, alright? I need some coffee. I feel just kind of down a little bit. So anyway, so ok, you're gonna talk to the coach . . . do you think maybe she should finish the season or will we fire her after the season or should we just do that right now?
Principal:	Oh, I think that's what you, ah, you know if you wanna pursue that more, I think you have to talk to our AD about that, ah Bill . . . .(phone rings)
Superintendent:	Sorry . . . Ah, just ignore this one. She'll get the idea. Anyway, talk to Bill about the AD . . . well, we kind of talked about that, he knows how I feel. You know, he knows we . . . Yeah, you know if she would just do a little bit better job with the strategy or something, These kids gotta be so frustrated. You know, and they're not gonna go anywhere and ah . . . if Megan were doing more than playing in the back row I think it would make a huge difference but, ah, she really ought to be in there all the time. You can't tell me a 5'1" girl can't spike. You know, I know she can spike. Well, you know she can spike, you've seen her do it, so . . .
Principal:	Yeah. I've seen her.

Superintendent:	You know, so I think it's something we ought to really take a, you know, look at right now, but I, you know, the AD, he's pretty worthless too, don't you think? I don't know . . .
Principal:	No, what I think we probably need to do . . .
Superintendent:	Marge, where's that coffee?
Principal:	What I think we probably need to do is wait 'til the season plays out. We've got the conference tournament next week . . . see where that goes.
Superintendent:	Oh, no, no, no. She's a senior, man. There's no time left for her. What's she gonna do, she won't get her scholarship, she was gonna be a scholarship player . . . Ah, that's just not gonna work, so bad idea. What's your next idea?
Principal:	Ah, I think that is the idea. The best idea that I can come up with . . .
Superintendent:	Well, you've had twelve hours to think about this. I mean we talked about this last night, so you know, you should have a, you should have better ideas than that. Wait 'til the end of the season, I don't like that one. So, you think maybe we should go ahead and get her fired then?
Principal:	No, I think this probably comes into more of an issue of you as dad, as opposed to you as (superintendent). Maybe you need to come in and talk to her, you know, talk to coach, maybe have your daughter come in and talk to coach . . . and kind of go . . . You remember how we, last year, we had all those steps to follow . . . if you have an issue with a coach, step one, kid talks to the coach . . .
Superintendent:	Yeah, I was out of line last year, I'll give you that. I was way over the top last year, but you know, that's not happening now. I've been pretty good up to this point, I think. But, I just can't watch it any more. I just really can't. Yeah, I think you're right, I think we ought to do something about it.
Principal:	I think it's just following those rules we set up . . . as how the level of hierarchy, how you approach a situation . . . I think we have to follow it just like every other parent needs to follow those, and go that way and see if we can make some head road . . .
Superintendent:	Well, other parents feel the same way I do. Most of them are coming and telling me Megan ought to be playing more and if she did, that would make a huge difference. I mean, I've got a lot of them that would say that. Yeah. Don't you agree? Don't you think that's the way it should be?
Principal:	I don't know. I mean, I've got so many other things to worry about and I wasn't aware of those . . .
Superintendent:	Oh, this isn't important to you?

Principal:	Oh, it's important to me and I'm all for the fine arts and the athletics altogether but I think coach has the . . .
Superintendent:	Fine arts, yeah. Whatever.
Principal:	I think coach has the, ah, best chance to see what all the gals do every day in practice . . .
Superintendent:	Well, you're there in practice. I'm there in practice. We've sat there and watched practice together, you know, and I thought we both agreed on this but maybe not, so, but . . . So now, what do you think? I'll listen.
Principal:	I think we just need to go through those steps, um and you know, if you see something that . . .
Superintendent:	Marge, I've not seen that coffee yet!
Principal:	You know, when she gets here, maybe we can talk about it together or I can talk with her about it. And see what she feels. Maybe get her end of it, too. See how she's feeling . . .
Superintendent:	Who's that you're talking about? The coach?
Principal:	Your daughter.
Superintendent:	Oh, the daughter. Yeah, well, Jeez, she can't even walk to school for Heaven's sake. I don't know if she's . . . I don't know . . . This is more I think about me and the coach probably, don't you think? Or more about . . . ah, I don't know. Yeah, you can talk to her if you want. She's got a pretty good head on her shoulders . . . she's kind of needy but . . .

DISCUSSION AND REFLECTION QUESTIONS

1. Identify the key issue(s).
2. Identify the secondary issue(s).
3. How should Principal Smock respond to Dr. Horn's complaint about the clothes Marge (the principal's secretary) is wearing?
4. Throughout this scenario, Dr. Horn demonstrates that he either is not listening to what Principal Smock says or simply turns what the principal says around to fit his own agenda. Evaluate Principal Smock's communication with the superintendent. Does he effectively identify the main issue that has Dr. Horn upset?
5. At 1:06:36 Dr. Horn raises the issue of firing the volleyball coach. Principal Smock suggests that the superintendent talk with Bill, the activities director. In this exchange, does Principal Smock fail to adequately support the volleyball coach? Shortly after, Dr. Horn comments that the activities director is "pretty worthless too . . . " Does Principal Smock have an obligation to defend the activities director to Dr. Horn? Would it

make any difference? Is it unprofessional of Dr. Horn to bad mouth the activities director to Principal Smock?

6. At 1:08:05 Dr. Horn again raises the question of firing the volleyball coach. Principal Smock responds that he thinks the issue is between Dr. Horn as a father, his daughter, and the coach. Principal Smock then refers to steps that were established last year for questions related to student-athletes' playing time. Is this an effective strategy?

7. At 1:09:08 Dr. Horn shifts the conversation back to his daughter's playing time and questions whether the issue is important to the principal. Evaluate Principal Smock's response. Given Dr. Horn's frustration and personality, should Principal Smock be concerned about his own standing with the superintendent?

8. Near the end of the scenario, Principal Smock suggests that he and Dr. Horn might talk with Megan about her feelings. Principal Smock also suggests that he might talk with Dr. Horn's daughter himself. Is this a good suggestion? Or does it inappropriately entangle the principal in an issue that should be handled by others? If Principal Smock should not be involved, who should address this?

9. Does Principal Smock have an obligation to address the way Dr. Horn communicates with Marge?

10. The scenario ends without closure. Describe the actions you would take as principal.

11. When observing difficult or unethical supervisors, aspiring principals often say they would not be able to work with such a leader and would simply have to seek other opportunities. And this may indeed be the best course of action. However, the situation becomes much more complicated with considering other factors such as:

   • That our spouse/significant other may be in his/her dream job;
   • That it may not be economically feasible to move;
   • That, professionally speaking, we need to stay in our current position for at least a couple of years;
   • That our own children may be well-established with their school and friends and a move would not be in their best interest.

   At the same time, to deal with a supervisor like this can certainly take a toll. How might Principal Smock effectively deal with Dr. Horn's behavior and style? Since the superintendent seems to have little use for the volleyball coach or Bill, the activities director, should Principal Smock be concerned that he might also be a target of Dr. Horn's ire at some point?

12. Given Dr. Horn's personality and unwillingness to listen, does Principal Smock engage in a skillful strategy of letting him talk? Or does Principal

Smock allow Dr. Horn to twist his words and control too much of the conversation? Explain.

13. Identify areas in which you believe the principal acted effectively.
14. Identify areas in which you believe the principal could have acted more effectively.

Balcony View

Generally speaking, how did the principal perform in this scenario? What would you have done differently?

Standards In Action

Which standards do you see as relevant in the scenario? Does the principal effectively meet them? Are there standards and/or criteria left unmet by the principal's actions?

Self Check

Picturing yourself in the principal's chair, describe your emotions. Does the case touch any of your biases or prior experiences?

Switch It Up

How might your thinking or approach change if the gender, social class, ethnicity, language, age, sexual orientation or other descriptors of the players involved were different?

Principal's Presence

In televised presidential debates, "looking presidential" is an important measure of a candidate's performance. The same is true for principals. Halpern and Lubar (2003, p. 3) define leadership presence as being more than "commanding attention" to include "the ability to connect authentically with the thoughts and feelings of others." Does the principal exert an effective "Principal's Presence?" Explain.

Principal's Priority

How *serious* is the situation?
How *soon* should the principal address this situation?

In A Word

Capture the principal's performance in the scenario using one word.

Collaborate

Collaborate with a classmate or colleague to rewrite or alter the case with a different set of circumstances. Share your new case with other colleagues to ascertain how they would approach it.

Extension & Internship Experiences

- Examine your school or district protocol related to questions related to student-athletes' playing time. Are the policies and procedures well-communicated and understood by students, parents, coaches, and administrators? Is the division of responsibility clear? Are policies or guidelines in place to address potential conflicts of interest?
- Examine your school or district policy related to the evaluation of coaches and extra-curricular sponsors. Are evaluations performed on a regular and formal basis? Determine whether coaching and extra-curricular contracts are separate from teaching contracts and the conditions under which coach and sponsor contracts may be terminated or not renewed.
- Does your school or district offer coaches and sponsors professional development or guidance related to effective communication with parents and community members?

REFERENCES AND RESOURCES

Blase, J. (2009). School administrator mistreatment of teachers. *International Handbook of Research on Teachers and Teaching: Springer International Handbooks of Education, 21*(5), 433–448. doi: 10.1007/978-0-387-73317-3_28

Blase, J., & Blase, J. (2002). The dark side of leadership: Teacher perspectives of principal mistreatment. *Education Administration Quarterly, 38*(5), 671–727.

Blase, J., & Blase, J. (2003). *Breaking the silence: Overcoming the problem of principal mistreatment of teachers.* Thousand Oaks, CA: Corwin Press.

Blase, J., Blase, J., & Du, F. (2008). The mistreated teacher: A national study. *Journal of Educational Administration, 46*(3), 263–301.

Kowalski, T. J. (2012). *Case studies on educational administration.* (6th ed.). Upper Saddle River, NJ: Pearson.

Rayner, C., Hoel, H., & Cooper, C. L. (2002). *Workplace bullying: What we know, who is to blame, and what can we do?* London, England: Taylor & Francis.

Tschannen-Moran, M., & Hoy, W. (1998). Trust in schools: A conceptual and empirical analysis. *Journal of Education Administration, 36*(4), 334–352. doi: 10.1108/09578239810211518

Waite, D., & Allen, D. (2003). Corruption and abuse of power in educational administration. *The Urban Review, 35*(4), 281–296. doi: 10.1023/B:URRE.0000017531.73129.4f

West, C. E., & Darrington, M. L. (2009). *Leadership teaming: The principal-superintendent relationship.* Thousand Oaks, CA: Corwin Press.

Whitaker, T. (2003). *What great principals do differently: Fifteen things that matter most.* Larchmont, NY: Eye on Education.

Hot Seat #13

Do You Support My Program? (Middle School)

Mr. Cox has taught Spanish at Hoover Middle School for twenty years. His program has steadily grown in size and currently enrolls more than 150 students, many of whom actively participate in the Spanish Club. In recent years, the group's Cinco de Mayo celebration has become a staple of springtime festivities at Hoover.

On the afternoon of May 4, Mr. Cox catches Principal Dan Scannell in his office with a complaint. Mr. Cox has gotten wind of a rumor that a number of students are planning a protest of the Cinco de Mayo celebration. Mr. Cox believes that three other teachers are promoting the protest, largely out of jealousy. He complains that their bitterness and envy of his successful program has driven some colleagues toward sabotage. With little time to spare before the end of the day, Principal Scannell pieces together the story and tries to formulate a plan.

Teaching can be an isolated, lonely endeavor. Schedules, class size and a tradition of working alone produce what amounts to a culture of isolation in many schools. Where isolation flourishes, relationships are hard to nurture. Payne (2008, p. 35) cited work by the Consortium on Chicago School Research that concluded "the quality of relationships among adults determined much of what did or did not happen in schools." Hoy, Gage III, and Tarter (2006), Hoy, Tarter and Witkoskie (1992), and others have pointed to the importance of trust among teachers and principals.

Professional Learning Communities (PLC) have gained considerable momentum as educators work to break the traditional bonds of teacher isolation and lack of trust. DuFour, DuFour, Eaker and Karhanek (2004, p. 2) noted that educators in PLCs recognize that "the fundamental purpose of school is learning, not teaching." In a similar vein, Sergiovanni and Starratt

(2007) described "communities of practice" in which teachers come together in a common effort to help each other teach, and learn, to care for each other and to work together in advancing student academic achievement" (p. 5).

On the eve of the annual Cinco de Mayo celebration, Mr. Cox has Principal Scannell wondering if this is possible in his school. Before the end of the day, he needs to decide on a course of action, because the celebration and rumored walkout are tomorrow.

THE TRANSCRIPT

Teacher:	Dan, you got a second?
Principal:	Yeah, Mr. Cox. How are you doing?
Teacher:	I've been better.
Principal:	You wanna have a seat someplace . . . here or over there?
Teacher:	I don't know. I'm kind of mad. I don't know if I wanna sit just yet.
Principal:	Ok.
Teacher:	You've heard . . . you now about my big Cinco de Mayo celebration picnic that we do every year.
Principal:	Yeah, definitely.
Teacher:	Well, you know, we talked about that at team leaders . . .
Principal:	Ok.
Teacher:	. . . and no one ever said a word and now today, ah, you know the thing's gonna be tomorrow and today I start finding out from kids that there's some teachers trying to sabotage this.
Principal:	Oh, wow.
Teacher:	So, I . . . I am gonna sit.
Principal:	Ok, that'd be great and we can sit over here or if you want something to write on.
Teacher:	Ah, I'll sit here.
Principal:	That's fine. Alrighty. Well, I, ah, that's frustrating. That's frustrating.
Teacher:	It is frustrating! And I guess first of all, I've gotta know do you support my program here?
Principal:	The Cinco de Mayo celebration?
Teacher:	The Cinco de Mayo and the Spanish program, 'cause . . .
Principal:	I think, ah, I think that Cinco de Mayo culturally is a really important event in that, ah, in your program and it's important to recognize and pursue and see how that might play into our curriculum. Um, tell me a little bit more about where you feel you're getting resistance.
Teacher:	Well, because there's ah, three teachers trying to stage a walkout tomorrow because they're pissed.

Principal:	Alright.
Teacher:	Jealous . . . I don't know what they are. But they're mad that ah, you know, twenty years I've been here at Hoover and we've done this every year and haven't had any issues . . . Five principals, they've all been supportive and now, ah, a couple of newer teachers and some ones that are just cranky and suddenly this is a big issue . . . So I . . .
Principal:	Ok.
Teacher:	Sorry, I had to jot down some notes cause I was too mad and I was sure I'd miss something.
Principal:	Ok.
Teacher:	Ah, I even hesitated. I didn't know if I should tell you who they were but I'm just irritated enough that I think you need to know who they are.
Principal:	Well, I'll tell you. You know what, kind a walking in, I'd be frustrated with the information that I got that somebody was trying to, ah, maybe dismember one of the activities I was doing . . .
Teacher:	Darn right!
Principal:	But I would like to know the names of those teachers so that we can talk to them and kind of see where they're coming from and maybe what their concerns are and see where we can get with that.
Teacher:	Alright. Ah, the first one's Mrs. Johnson.
Principal:	Ok.
Teacher:	Math teacher.
Principal:	Do you mind if I . . . ?
Teacher:	No go ahead. You need my pen?
Principal:	And I can even take that when you're done with it, if that's possible.
Teacher:	Yep, that'd be fine.
Principal:	Alright, well let's just lead with that.
Teacher:	Well, she's mad, first of all, that you put her on that plan of assistance two months ago.
Principal:	Ok.
Teacher:	And you know, kids just run wild in that classroom as it is and everybody knows it and she just cries or yells, or I don't know . . .
Principal:	And do you know, her mentor is . . .
Teacher:	Mrs. Jordan . . .
Principal:	Ok, alright, well . . .
Teacher:	But, it's a lost cause. You know that, you're in and out of there every day as it is. But she's mad because it's gonna make kids miss math supplemental time to be part of this picnic tomorrow and she's afraid that that's just one more reason you're gonna fire her cause they're gonna miss more math

	time and she won't put up with that. So, that's something that you're gonna have to deal with and then there's Mr. Williams, the band director.
Principal:	Ok.
Teacher:	And, ah, he's irritated that kids are gonna miss some band lessons . . .
Principal:	Ok.
Teacher:	. . . you know, like that's the end of the world. Ah, doesn't agree with your new arrangement that, you know, they can't get pulled out of math and reading to go to band lessons and . . .
Principal:	Yeah.
Teacher:	I sure would like to only have to teach, you know, a little bit during the day with one group of kids and then have three or four the rest of the day, but that's not how it works.
Principal:	Yeah.
Teacher:	Ah, Mrs. Smith, she's the other one and this is a shocker because she's our ELL teacher.
Principal:	Yeah.
Teacher:	But, she's got a bee in her bonnet because she thinks we should have a Bosnian celebration instead of a Spanish one. Now I know there's a hundred and fifty Bosnian kids here and there's fifty Spanish kids, but we don't teach Bosnian. We teach Spanish.
Principal:	Yeah, I agree and but at the same time, you know, we can always explore the possibility . . .
Teacher:	Ok.
Principal:	We have a lot of different ethnicities that come through our building and I think you being a Spanish teacher would really empathize with wanting to, you know, see those students have their faces and cultures represented . . .
Teacher:	Oh, of course! But . . . I would think so.
Principal:	. . . in our curriculum and you may be even able to give some pointers into some kind of a celebration of their culture because of your familiarity with doing that with Cinco de Mayo.
Teacher:	I don't want her sabotaging this big event that we've got going on.
Principal:	Oh, no. We don't want that.
Teacher:	Well here's what I think you need to do. I think you need to get on the PA and make an all-school announcement.
Principal:	Ok.
Teacher:	And I even wrote one for you as a sample . . .
Principal:	I do certainly appreciate that. Do you mind if I take a look at it and kind of . . .
Teacher:	No, and I put it in all caps because I think you should talk loud when you make this announcement.
Principal:	Well, I usually do. The kids think I'm nuts . . .

Teacher:	Well, I know but I think you really need to talk loud cause, you know, if they're up in Mrs. Johnson's room they aren't gonna hear it unless they are talking loud. But you need to do that and you need to do this today because the picnic is tomorrow . . .
Principal:	Ok.
Teacher:	So you think you might do that at the end of this period or at the end of the day, or . . .
Principal:	We've still got some time to kind of . . . What I . . . I'll be honest with you. You know, I'm equally concerned that there may be some conflict among staff members about an event that we've got planned and is on the schedule . . .
Teacher:	Right.
Principal:	And so I do want to pursue that a little bit . . . we've been working with her to see what kinds of supports we can provide in there . . . and so I'd like to talk with some of those teachers and kind of see where they're coming from and . . .
Teacher:	Well, I've got two more things I want you to do.
Principal:	Oh, definitely. I can hear those.
Teacher:	I want you to write up those teachers, cause they can't be trying to wreck this event. That's like insubordination or something. I know you'll find something somewhere to write them up.
Principal:	Yeah.
Teacher:	And, ah, I think that your two assistant principals and the SRO (School Resource Officer) should patrol the hallways tomorrow to make sure no kids walk out of class to try to stage this, you know, big protest.
Principal:	Well . . .
Teacher:	And, so if they're out in the hallways, you know, if you're not in eighth grade you don't come out to go to the party during any other time and you just keep some control here. I think that's what we need to do . . . So there's my notes.
Principal:	Well, you know, I do, ah, I appreciate you stopping in and sharing that with me and coming here rather than, so, you know, we can approach this maybe together and see how we can resolve that.
Teacher:	So when am I gonna know when you're gonna do this stuff?
Principal:	Well, again, I want to have some conversations with people and . . .
Teacher:	Ok, but it's tomorrow.
Principal:	Yeah, I recognize that. And we've got the afternoon to kind of explore what's happening and see what's going on. I don't know that there's a problem with an announcement that kind of lets them know that the celebration is tomorrow and that we're supportive . . .
Teacher:	And that you support it . . . Cause I want to make sure that . . . teachers understand that.

Principal:	I can get behind it and be supportive of it, yeah . . . We'll enjoy that celebration with the kids too.
Teacher:	Alright
Principal:	But I do. I wanna hear what our other teachers are concerned with and see if there's a way to maybe help with their understanding or see how they can be participating in it or, you know, I really like the idea of a Bosnian celebration. I think that that's a group of kids that needs to see themselves represented so they can be engaged more in school and it's early on, I know you're frustrated . . .

DISCUSSION AND REFLECTION QUESTIONS

1. Identify the key issue(s).
2. Identify the secondary issue(s).
3. At 1:11:03 Mr. Cox asks the principal if he supports the Spanish program and Cinco de Mayo Celebration. Evaluate Principal Scannell's answer.
4. At 1:12:10 Principal Scannell says he would be frustrated to hear that a colleague might be trying to "sabotage" an activity.
5. At 1:12:24 Mr. Cox accuses three other teachers of trying to sabotage the Cinco de Mayo celebration. Evaluate Principal Scannell's response.
6. As Mr. Cox explains what he believes to be the reasons the three teachers object to the celebration, it becomes clear that he has his own issues with the teachers. Evaluate the principal's response to what Mr. Cox says are their reasons. Is it inappropriate for Mr. Cox to say what he says about his colleagues? Should Principal Scannell have addressed these comments with Mr. Cox or simply listen to get a full picture?
7. What do you think of Principal Scannell's suggestion that a Bosnian celebration might be a good idea? Should he raise this with Mr. Cox or wait until he has talked with the other teachers? Explain.
8. Anticipate Mrs. Johnson's reaction if she learns that Principal Scannell and Mr. Cox discussed her classroom, her plan of assistance, and the principal's assertion that "she struggles a bit." How would you respond if you were Mrs. Johnson? How should Principal Scannell respond when confronted by Mrs. Johnson?
9. Mr. Cox identifies a number of actions he wants the principal to take, including reading the announcement he wrote over the intercom and having patrols in the hallway. Evaluate Principal Scannell's response to the things Mr. Cox wants done. How would you respond to a teacher asking, suggesting or telling you what to do in a case like this? Is Mr. Cox out of line in asking when Principal Scannell will take action? Or is he simply concerned because the celebration is tomorrow?

10. Does Principal Scannell adequately address the possibility of a walkout or disruption tomorrow? If he learns that the three teachers have overtly (or implicitly) encouraged some kind of student protest or walkout, what action should he take with students? With teachers?
11. Identify areas in which you believe the principal acted effectively.
12. Identify areas in which you believe the principal could have acted more effectively.

Balcony View

Generally speaking, how did the principal perform in this scenario? What would you have done differently?

Standards In Action

Which standards do you see as relevant in the scenario? Does the principal effectively meet them? Are there standards and/or criteria left unmet by the principal's actions?

Self Check

Picturing yourself in the principal's chair, describe your emotions. Does the case touch any of your biases or prior experiences?

Switch It Up

How might your thinking or approach change if the gender, social class, ethnicity, language, age, sexual orientation or other descriptors of the players involved were different?

Principal's Presence

In televised presidential debates, "looking presidential" is an important measure of a candidate's performance. The same is true for principals. Halpern and Lubar (2003, p. 3) define leadership presence as being more than "commanding attention" to include "the ability to connect authentically with the thoughts and feelings of others." Does the principal exert an effective "Principal's Presence?" Explain.

Principal's Priority

How *serious* is the situation?

How *soon* should the principal address this situation?
Should the principal inform/involve a *supervisor* on this issue?

In A Word

Capture the principal's performance in the scenario using one word.

Collaborate

Collaborate with a classmate or colleague to rewrite or alter the case with a different set of circumstances. Share your new case with other colleagues to ascertain how they would approach it.

Extension & Internship Experiences

- Examine your school or district policy on curriculum-related celebrations, such as the Cinco de Mayo picnic described by Mr. Cox. What is the process for proposing a similar event, such as the Bosnian celebration discussed in the case? What are the standards by which such activities are judged to be educationally relevant?
- Discuss with a mentor the most effective techniques for managing conflict between teachers and any lessons learned the hard way.

REFERENCES AND RESOURCES

Blase, J., & Kirby, P. C. (2009). *Bringing out the best in teachers: What effective principals do.* (3rd ed.). Thousand Oaks, CA: Corwin Press.

Brock, B. L., & Grady, M. L. (2009). *From difficult teachers to dynamic teams.* Thousand Oaks, CA: Corwin Press.

DuFour, R. (2007). Professional learning communities: A bandwagon, an idea worth considering, or our best hope for high levels of learning?. *Middle School Journal, 39*(1), 4–8.

DuFour, R., DuFour, R., & Eaker, A. (2008). *Revisiting professional learning communities: New insights for improving schools.* Bloomington, IN: Solution Tree Press.

DuFour, R., DuFour, R., Eaker, R., & Karhanek, G. (2004). *Whatever it takes. How professional learning communities respond when kids don't learn.* Bloomington, IN: National Educational Service.

Fogarty, R., & Pete, B. (2009). Professional Learning 101. *Phi Delta Kappan, 91*(4), 32–34. Retrieved from EBSCO*host.*

Hipp, K., Huffman, J., Pankake, A. M., & Olivier, D. F. (2008). Sustaining professional learning communities: Case studies. *Journal of Educational Change, 9*(2), 173–195. doi: 10.1007/s10833-007-9060-8

Hord, S. M., Roussin, J. L., & Sommers, W. A. (2009). Guiding professional learning communities: Inspiration, challenge, surprise, and meaning. Thousand Oaks, CA: Corwin Press.

Hoy, W. K., Gage III, C., & Tarter, C. (2006). School Mindfulness and Faculty Trust: Necessary Conditions for Each Other?. *Educational Administration Quarterly, 42*(2), 236–255. doi: 10.1177/0013161X04273844

Hoy, W. K., Tarter, C., & Witkoskie, L. (1992). Faculty trust in colleagues: Linking the principal with school effectiveness. *Journal of Research & Development in Education, 38*. Retrieved from EBSCO*host*.

McEwan, E. K. (2005). *Dealing with teachers who are angry, troubled, exhausted, or just plain confused*. Thousand Oaks, CA: Corwin Press.

Payne, C. M. (2010). *So much reform, so little change: The persistence of failure in urban schools*. Cambridge, MA: Harvard Education Press.

Sergiovanni, T. J., & Starratt, R. J. (2007). *Supervision: A redefinition*. New York, NY: McGraw-Hill.

Servage, L. (2009). Who is the "professional" in a professional learning community? An exploration of teacher professionalism in collaborative professional development settings. *Canadian Journal of Education, 32*(1), 149–171. Retrieved from EBSCO*host*.

Spanneut, G. (2010). Professional learning communities: Principals and collegial conversations. *Kappa Delta Pi Record, 46*(3), 100–3. Retrieved from Education Full Text database.

Whitaker, T. (2002). *Dealing with difficult teachers*. (2nd Ed.). Larchmont, NY: Eye on Education.

Hot Seat #14

He Needs To Back Off!
(High School)

We all know the extraordinary impact teachers can have on students' lives. Many of us can describe teachers and coaches who've impacted our lives in immeasurable ways. We also know that sometimes, teacher-student relationships cross the line. Although official records are difficult to come by, few incidents of teacher misconduct have attracted as much attention as the case of Mary Kay Letourneau, the Washington State teacher convicted of having sexual relations with a 13 year-old student. Similar high profile cases have bought a spotlight to the dangers of teacher-student relationships gone awry.

Enter Mr. Coulter, the father of an eleventh grade girl who serves as a manager for the varsity boys' basketball team. Mr. Coulter, a polite but testy man, comes to Principal Jones' office unannounced. He wastes no time in telling Principal Jones that the basketball coach, a good-looking man in his early twenties, needs to leave his daughter alone. When asked by Principal Jones what specifically the coach has been doing, Mr. Coulter describes text messages, rides home from practice, and physical closeness his daughter has experienced. While Principal Jones gives his word that he takes the situation seriously, Mr. Coulter wants to know exactly what action will be taken and when.

In 2004 a little-known U.S. Department of Education report authored by Charol Shakeshaft revealed disturbing statistics on teacher-student relationships. Shakeshaft (2004, p. 18) estimated that "more than 4.5 million students are subject to some form of sexual abuse by an employee of a school sometime between kindergarten and 12th grade." As cited in Hendrie (2004, para. 8), Shakeshaft's statement that "the physical sexual abuse of students in schools is likely more than 100 times the abuse by priests" sparked alarm, as well as criticism from the National Education Association, which charged that the figure represented "a misuse of data" (Hendrie, 2004, para. 9).

While the actual number of abuse cases may never be known, other research has concluded that abuse by educators is probably underreported for a host of reasons, including a desire to avoid negative publicity and liability (Fauske, Mullen, & Sutton, 2006). Shakeshaft and Cohan (1995) found that 7.5 percent of superintendents who had investigated alleged abuse cases ultimately determined the accusations to be false or were not serious enough to be considered sexual abuse. The authors, however, pointed out that while some accusations were not as serious as some parents alleged or failed to constitute sexual abuse in the superintendents' judgments, the teachers' actions were still likely illegal. The authors concluded that false allegations represent a small portion of the total. Additionally, Hassenpflug and Riggs (1996) noted that accused teachers also face severe repercussions, even when the allegations are false. The implications for all parties involved are formidable.

In this emotionally charged context, Principal Jones begins searching for answers.

THE TRANSCRIPT

Principal:	Hi, Mr. Coulter.
Dad:	How you doing?
Principal:	Good, how are you?
Dad:	Not real happy.
Principal:	Ok, what can I do for you?
Dad:	Your basketball coach needs to leave my daughter alone.
Principal:	Can you tell me what he's doing?
Dad:	Ah, let's see . . . He's sent her a few text messages. She's a manager on the varsity basketball team, she's a junior, and ah, he sent her some text messages just saying hi, wondering what's going on . . . He's given her a ride home from practice a couple times. I've put a stop to that. She's not getting anywhere near his car. Um, she told me that a couple times he's come up and put his arm around her shoulder . . . once or twice put his arm around her waist. He's being too close and needs to back the hell up. What are you gonna do?
Principal:	Do you have copies of the text messages that I can take a look at?
Dad:	I can get them.
Principal:	Ok. I'd appreciate taking a look at those. I will definitely call your daughter in and have a conversation with her . . . I'm gonna have a conversation with him as well.
Dad:	What about your basketball coach? I'll get my daughter cleared up. That's not a problem. What about him?

Principal:	I'd like to get the facts from all different sides. I hear your story now. I'd like to hear her story and then I'd like to bring him in and find out what's going on from his perspective.
Dad:	Because I know that one or two of the other players on the team that are her friends have also told me in a roundabout way that something looks funky. And if I keep hearing this stuff, then it might get a little bit ugly. He needs to stay away from her. I realize he's twenty-three, twenty-four, young guy, good-looking guy, whatever. He needs to leave my daughter alone, otherwise things are gonna get ugly.
Principal:	I can assure you that I'm gonna get to the bottom of this . . . without a doubt . . .
Dad:	How?
Principal:	Like I said, I'm gonna call everybody in and make sure that I understand the full side of the story . . . it sounds to me . . .
Dad:	And what if he kind of puts that little intimidation factor, "hey, shh, don't talk to him, nothing's wrong . . . " Then what?
Principal:	I'll make sure that I have a conversation with the young ladies before I call him in, before he knows that I'm conducting an investigation to find out what's going on. And I'll also call in the basketball players who are a part of the team who have observed the same behaviors that you're observing so that I can speak with them confidentially and privately before he . . .
Dad:	Then how are you gonna keep that, keep that from getting out?
Principal:	A lot of behaviors . . . .
Dad:	How are you gonna trust sixteen, seventeen year old boys not to go, "Hey, coach is messing with Avery and now he's in trouble." How are you gonna keep that from getting out? Cause it will. I promise. And then all of the sudden you got a whole bunch of folks mad at her because they all like him. And she didn't do anything except wanting to help out.
Principal:	Well, we'll call them in and try to make sure that it's as confidential as possible and we're gonna get to the bottom of it right away. Starting as soon as we're done with our conversation here, I'll begin calling people in to find out what's going on and to make sure that they have an opportunity to tell me what's going on honestly. I'm very concerned about the behaviors that you've explained to me . . .
Dad:	You better be. Cause very quickly, it's gonna go whoosh . . . right over the top of your head to somebody else and I'll keep going because . . .
Principal:	Sure . . .
Dad:	. . . he needs to leave my daughter alone.
Principal:	I agree. If the behavior is inappropriate, then, ah, there will be some consequences for the teacher . . .

Dad:	Such as?
Principal:	Well . . .
Dad:	Like what?
Principal:	We need to make sure of that, ah, what you're describing to me is accurate.
Dad:	You gonna fire him?
Principal:	Potentially, that could be something . . .
Dad:	Gonna have him charged?
Principal:	We'll look at the evidence and find out what's going on and then we'll try to make a determination from there. Ah, it seems to me that obviously you're very concerned, I'm extremely concerned . . . about the situation, as well.
Dad:	Concerned? Pissed off! Pissed off would be a better word because . . .
Principal:	I understand that, Mr. Coulter.
Dad:	. . . if it's me and him in the same room . . . I might be old, but I'll go down swinging.
Principal:	Sure.
Dad:	Cause if he keeps messing, it's not gonna be pretty. So you better, you better fix it.
Principal:	We're gonna do everything in our power from preventing that situation from ever happening. And I can promise you that it will be handled appropriately . . .
Dad:	Don't make promises . . .
Principal:	It will be fixed. I'm making this promise to you because it's going to be a promise that's kept. That we're gonna, I'm gonna assure you that I'm gonna get to the bottom of this. I'm gonna find out what's going on. As a parent, I would be, if I were in your shoes I would be beyond concerned as well. I understand the concern, the anger and the frustration . . .
Dad:	You're lucky that my wife convinced me to come here instead of go straight there, because otherwise we'd have had a different type of situation on our hands because I kind of put up with it, told her to stay away from him . . . this, that, and the other thing. She likes basketball, she can't play basketball herself so she wants to help out somehow. And this is not right. And you're lucky that my wife has a cooler head than me, bringing me here instead of going right to him and it might have gotten weird.
Principal:	I definitely appreciate you coming to me . . .
Dad:	So you have two days. Today is day one. By five o'clock tomorrow, I want some answers.
Principal:	I can assure you, like I said before, I can assure you that I'm gonna get to the bottom of this as quickly as possible and as soon as I find out all the facts, I'll contact you and be in contact with you right away.

Dad:	And what if you find out that, yeah, he is doing all this stuff? Then what?
Principal:	The consequences for the basketball coach will be appropriate to what's happened.
Dad:	Is he gonna be done? Cause she's staying.
Principal:	We need to find out what's going on first.
Dad:	She's staying with the team.
Principal:	We need to find out what's happening first and then we'll go from there. So, right now, unless you have anything further that you can add to my understanding of what's happening, maybe we can just leave our conversation here and start to call people in . . .
Dad:	Have you gotten weird comments and things like that from other people?
Principal:	I have not.
Dad:	Cause, I, you know, you get your ear here and your ear here and you listen and you start to go, ah, naw, you dismiss it, dismiss it. But now all of the sudden it's come around to my daughter so I'm a little bit confused and a little bit confused and concerned that maybe . . . this ain't the first time.
Principal:	I have not heard these concerns before. And had I heard concerns like this before, I can assure you that they would have been thoroughly investigated . . .

DISCUSSION AND REFLECTION QUESTIONS

1. Identify the key issue(s).
2. Identify the secondary issue(s).
3. Mr. Coulter gets quickly to the point with the implication that the basketball coach is behaving inappropriately toward his daughter. Principal Jones asks for specifics and also if Mr. Coulter can produce the text messages that the coach allegedly sent to his daughter. Should Principal Jones immediately begin taking notes of the conversation? Or, does he effectively get Mr. Coulter talking about the situation and we can assume that Principal Jones takes detailed notes as soon as the conversation ends? Would the principal taking notes possibly interrupt the flow of the conversation?
4. Does your district have a stated policy regarding communication and interaction between employees and students? Does the policy address electronic communication such as text messages or social media? Does the policy address students riding in employees' vehicles?
5. Some would argue that school employees should take a vigilant stance on physical contact with students, transporting students in personal vehicles, and so on. Others, including some parents say things such as,

"if my child needs a hug, I hope someone at the school will give him/
her a hug."

Imagine that a coach has come to you asking for advice on whether
to provide a student manager like Mr. Coulter's daughter a ride home
after an away basketball game. What would you suggest?

6. At numerous points in the conversation, Mr. Coulter suggests that the
situation with the coach could get "weird" or "ugly" and implies that he
might react physically toward the coach. Does Principal Jones adequately
address this? Explain. If not, how would you respond?

7. At 1:18:43 Mr. Coulter asks the principal what can be done to prevent
the basketball coach from intimidating his daughter into keeping quiet.
Evaluate Principal Jones' response. Would you respond to the question
in the same way? How could a principal address the possibility that the
coach might try to use his influence in this way?

8. At 1:19:05 Mr. Coulter asks Principal Jones how he intends to keep the
investigation "from getting out" as he believes it inevitably will. Evaluate
the response to this concern. How would you respond?

Not surprisingly, Mr. Coulter then presses Principal Jones to say
whether the basketball coach will be fired if the allegations are shown to
be true. Evaluate Principal Jones' response.

9. At 1:20:25 Mr. Coulter again mentions the possibility of a physical
conflict with the basketball coach. Does Principal Jones effectively
address this? Explain.

10. At 1:21:49 Mr. Coulter says that his daughter is "staying." What do you
think Mr. Coulter means? That his daughter is staying at the school?
Continuing as a manager for the basketball team? Is it appropriate for
her to continue as a manager of the basketball team? Should Principal
Jones have suggested that Mr. Coulter's daughter cease her involvement
with the team, pending the investigation? Or would doing so potentially
punish and ostracize her?

11. Mr. Coulter demands answers by "five o'clock tomorrow." Is this
ultimatum appropriate? Should the principal be concerned that if he does
not provide Mr. Coulter with some kind of answer by that time that he
may act on his references to physical conflict with the coach? Or does
Mr. Coulter, understandably, simply want immediate action?

12. At 1:22:00 Principal Jones suggests the two end their conversation so he
can begin investigating. Should he have continued the conversation or
does bringing closure demonstrate that he is taking the situation seriously
and will immediately begin investigating?

13. Construct a specific, step-by-step plan and rationale for what Principal
Jones should do as soon as Mr. Coulter leaves the office.

14. The allegations in this case are certainly serious. How can Principal Jones approach them seriously while still respecting the basketball coach's reputation and due process rights?
15. Identify areas in which you believe the principal acted effectively.
16. Identify areas in which you believe the principal could have acted more effectively.

Balcony View

Generally speaking, how did the principal perform in this scenario? What would you have done differently?

Standards In Action

Which standards do you see as relevant in the scenario? Does the principal effectively meet them? Are there standards and/or criteria left unmet by the principal's actions?

Self Check

Picturing yourself in the principal's chair, describe your emotions. Does the case touch any of your biases or prior experiences?

Switch It Up

How might your thinking or approach change if the gender, social class, ethnicity, language, age, sexual orientation or other descriptors of the players involved were different?

Principal's Presence

In televised presidential debates, "looking presidential" is an important measure of a candidate's performance. The same is true for principals. Halpern and Lubar (2003, p. 3) define leadership presence as being more than "commanding attention" to include "the ability to connect authentically with the thoughts and feelings of others." Does the principal exert an effective "Principal's Presence?" Explain.

Principal's Priority

How *serious* is the situation?

How *soon* should the principal address this situation?
Should the principal inform/involve a *supervisor* on this issue?

In A Word

Capture the principal's performance in the scenario using one word.

Collaborate

Collaborate with a classmate or colleague to rewrite or alter the case with a different set of circumstances. Share your new case with other colleagues to ascertain how they would approach it.

Extension & Internship Experiences

- Ask the administrator in charge of personnel at your school or district to review the step-by-step plan and rationale you constructed in #11 above. Note any areas that you missed or neglected. Ask the administrator to share the relevant district policy for alleged abuse by school employees with you.
- Examine the laws in your state concerning relationships between school employees and students. Access records for educators who have lost their licenses and/or been imprisoned for inappropriate relationships.
- Conduct a search of records of alleged inappropriate relationships between educators and students that were later shown to be false.
- Discuss suggested steps a new principal should take in a case such as this with your school or district attorney.

REFERENCES AND RESOURCES

Cairns, S. S. (2006). *School principals' knowledge and understanding of educator sexualmisconduct against students* (Doctoral Dissertation). Retrieved fromhttp://scholarcommons.usf.edu/etd/2468.

Fauske, J. R., Mullen, C. A., & Sutton, L. C. (2006, November). *Educator sexual misconduct in schools: Implications for leadership preparation.* Paper presented at the 2006 University Council for Education Administration Convention, San Antonio TX. Retrieved from http://www.ucea.org/storage/convention/convention2006/proceedings/FauskeUCEA2006.pdf.

Fibkins, W. L. (2005). *Innocence denied: A guide to preventing sexual misconduct by teachers and coaches.* Lanham, MD: Rowman and Littlefield.

Hassenpflug, A., & Riggs, R. O. (1996). Guilty until proven innocent? Protecting the rights of school district employees. *West's Education Law Quarterly*, 225. Retrieved from EBSCO*host*.

Helpful hints for emergency school management. (2008). *U.S. Department of Education, 3*(2). Retrieved from http://rems.ed.gov/docs/HH_Vol3Issue2.pdf.

Hendrie, C. (2004). Sexual Abuse By Educators Is Scrutinized. *Education Week, 23*(26), 1–17. Retrieved from EBSCO*host*.

Irvine, M., & Tanner, R. (2007, October 1). AP: Sexual misconduct plagues U. S. schools. *The Washington Post.* Retrieved from http://www.washingtonpost.com/.

Shoop, R. J. (2004). *Sexual exploitation in schools: How to spot it and stop it.* Thousand Oaks, CA: Corwin Press.

Shakeshaft, C. (2004). *Educator sexual misconduct: A synthesis of existing literature.* Prepared for the US Department of Education Office of the Under Secretary Policy and Program Studies Service Doc#2004–09. Retrieved from http://www.ed.gov.

Shakeshaft, C., & Cohan, A. (1995). Sexual abuse of students by school personnel. *Phi Delta Kappan, 76*(7), 512–520.

Hot Seat #15

The Values We Need
(Middle School)

Dr. Lee is a well-spoken, prominent parent with a history of charitable contributions to the school and local organizations. A pillar of the community, she's respected, polite and knows how to leverage relationships to get things done. On a visit to Principal Moser's office, she explains her leadership role in a service club focused on improving the values of local youth. She has brought with her a curriculum package that she believes will support the school's efforts to address students' values and behavior using lessons from the Bible. Armed with good intentions, a pleasant demeanor and knowledge of federal law, she would like Principal Moser's support in infusing the materials into the school's curriculum.

Few issues in education generate as much controversy and confusion as the nature of the separation between church and state—or in this case, role of religion in public schools. Dunklee and Shoop (2006, p. 33) called this "the most unsettled legal question in public education." La Morte (2012) noted that many Americans have not understood why "government" does not allow school prayer, yet allows legislative sessions to begin with prayers; allows the word *God* in the Pledge of Allegiance and on legal tender; allows taking an oath on the Bible in a court of law; employs chaplains in the military. (p. 50)

Some people have interpreted this as contradictory and evidence of hostility to religion, or particularly Christianity.

To further complicate matters, many politicians have publicly railed against Court decisions related to religion in schools and the public square. Given local context and public opinion, this "may have even encouraged inadvertent lawlessness at the local level by boards of education, school administrators, teachers, or parents who did not feel compelled to obey a controversial decision" (La Morte, 2012, p. 50).

Other school leaders, concerned that teaching about the Bible might lack a secular purpose and instead be perceived as promoting Christianity, "shy away from endorsing Bible teaching for fear of inviting lawsuits" (Essex, 2012, p. 36). This reluctance to invite an application of the Lemon test (*Lemon v. Kurtzman,* 1971), which examines the secular educational intent of schools, fuels charges that public schools and school administrators are hostile to Christianity (or other faiths).

Despite political rhetoric, media attention and school administrators' angst about the height of the wall between church and state, "Court decisions have not banned Bible reading for nonsectarian reasons, such as the teaching of the history of religions and the study of comparative religions," (La Morte, 2012, p. 51). Though controversial, the "Bible may be taught in public schools as a part of the school's curriculum if it is not associated with any form of worship and it is taught objectively as part of a secular program" (Essex, 2012, p. 36). Further, the U.S. Supreme Court's ruling in *Stone v. Graham* (1980) affirmed what Dr. Lee told Principal Moser in this case: that the Bible *may be* used to teach issues surrounding history, civilization, and ethics.

Essex (2012, p. 37) offered the following guide for administrators facing Principal Moser's dilemma:

- The Bible must be taught objectively and in a strict secular manner.
- Teachers should not create a devotional (religious) atmosphere when teaching the Bible.
- Teachers assigned to teach the Bible as part of the school's secular program must be properly instructed on how and what to teach.
- School officials should formulate policies governing Bible teaching through the involvement of teachers, students, and where appropriate, parents and community leaders.
- Bible-teaching policies should be communicated effectively to teachers, students, and parents.

As Principal Moser responds to Dr. Lee's proposal, many questions come to mind. Among them are how to handle the request and if she's been invited to the front lines of the Culture Wars.

THE TRANSCRIPT

The principal greets Dr. Lee and invites her to take a seat . . .

Mom: You know, I have children in the school district, in your school in
            particular. And I am the head of an organization that has its sole

purpose in improving the values of the children in our schools. And we believe that one way to do that is to infuse the work in the schools with a particular Bible curriculum.

Principal: Alright.

Mom: So, I brought the Aha Bible Curriculum to you today and I want you to implement this in the classrooms . . .

Principal: Ok.

Mom: We know that most of our kids are all Christian so, you know, they should all adhere to this. We also believe that the values that are reflected in this are the values that all of our children should have. So I'd like to leave this with you today and I'd really like to have you implement that in your classes.

Principal: I really appreciate you coming in today. Ah, I do think it is absolutely wonderful that you're wanting to help build those values and character things with our students. Um, however, we are a public school, so I can't go and, ah, give these to students. It's kind of like pushing that on them and ah . . .

Mom: Well, you're gonna see that this is a curriculum . . .

Principal: Ok.

Mom: I, you know, our Bible initiative comes later in the year.

Principal: Ok.

Mom: This is a particular curriculum and the curriculum is a Bible curriculum and it's I know that by, ah, the federal law we can teach Bible in the schools. And I, we know that and I have the documentation for that and I have the Supreme Court ruling on that as well, so . . .

Principal: Would you mind taking that out and showing me a little bit about it . . . and we are explaining to students maybe some background and history on it versus teaching the religion . . . That's kind of a different thing . . . and so we can teach them, um, the history and how it relates but really not teaching the religious aspects of it . . . and that it's part of the curriculum.

Mom: Right . . . And that's what this is. This approaches, um, the Christian religion from a historical perspective and a cultural perspective . . .

Principal: Ok.

Mom: And so that's why we think that this is very appropriate curriculum for you to use and you know the books, you hear there is some technology tools in there. I would like you to implement this. Um, I was even thinking it might work really well in one of the history classes or one of the English classes.

Principal: It sounds like, ah, wonderful, wonderful materials. I'm wondering if I could, ah, take this packet or this box of things and look through it and then take it to our curriculum director and see if

that could somehow relate to our education and the things that
we're currently doing . . . Ah, so we're not pushing the religious
aspects on to students and that we are aligning with the law like
you said.

Mom: Right. Um, you know, I would like you to do that and I can leave
these materials with you . . .

Principal: Sure.

Mom: Ah, but I also would just like to say that, you know, our religion is
a great religion and we really need to adhere. It has great values in
it, it . . . it you know, it would help with the conflict that's going
on in the schools between the students now and then . . . and so
those values are, you know, just buried so well in that and they're
throughout all of that. So those values are very important values
and you know, our city and our nation as a whole, you know, are
a part of those values and those values are underpinning so much
of what we do. So I think that you would find that this would be
a very, very important piece to add to your curriculum.

Principal: Yeah and I'm wondering if it has some more aspects to them.
We're doing some Character Counts kinds of things so I'm
wondering if it would align with that. Um, could I give you my
business card and take your information too . . .

Mom: Yes.

Principal: . . . and once I can go through the materials and make sure that,
like you said, we're aligning with what the law would say . . . and
then step forward if we can . . . I don't want to make promises
with you but I would really like to look through the materials and
they sound wonderful and I really like the technology aspect in it
too because we definitely have great technology today and would
hope to, ah . . .

Mom: Well, you know, I can leave these with you today . . .

Principal: Ok, that would be great.

Mom: And, ah, do you know when you might get back with me?

Principal: Um, could I say about a week or so? Ah, I know the curriculum
director is very, very busy . . . And I don't want to do and push
things on her right away, but it would give me time to look
through the things and then meet with her and kind of go from
there. And I can . . . I'll give you a call within a week to let you
know where we're at with that and my thoughts on the curriculum
and just explain . . .

Mom: And I would expect you to push this a little bit because this is what
our kids need. We know that. We know that we need to do this. And
we know the values are there. We know, ah, that this is a historical
and cultural perspective and we know this is what our students need
and we would expect you to push that into your curriculum . . .

DISCUSSION AND REFLECTION QUESTIONS

1. Identify the key issue(s).
2. Identify the secondary issue(s).
3. After Principal Moser explains that she works in a public school and cannot be "pushing" a particular religion, Dr. Lee explains that the materials she has brought constitute an organized curriculum. She also refers to federal law and a Supreme Court case that allows for the Bible to be taught in public schools. Evaluate Principal Moser's response. Would you respond differently? If so, why?
4. After Dr. Lee refers to court rulings (1:24:04), does it appear at that Principal Moser is more receptive to considering and reviewing the materials? Or do you believe she is simply and politely listening to Dr. Lee's argument?
5. At 1:25:00 Principal Moser uses the word "wonderful" to describe the materials. Does this imply that she agrees with Dr. Lee that the materials would likely be an important addition to the school's curriculum? Or is she simply making polite conversation? Does Principal Moser's suggestion that she will examine the materials and discuss them with the curriculum director imply that she intends to support their infusion into the curriculum? Would you have responded differently? If so, how and why?
6. At 1:26:11 Principal Moser references the school's existing Character Counts program. Evaluate. Does her response intimate that she believes the materials might align with the school's current practice?

   Many schools teach character and values through a host of programs, such as Character Counts. How should a principal respond to a stakeholder who asserts that a particular curriculum simply reinforces what is already being taught, but in a way that reflects the community's prevailing values and faith?
7. Should Principal Moser initiate a conversation about the Aha curriculum with the curriculum director? Is she obligated to do this since she told Dr. Lee she would do so? Is she likely wasting the curriculum director's time?

   Assuming the Aha Bible Curriculum is not infused into the school's program, will it appear that the curriculum director is the reason? Could this create problems for Principal Moser? Or is it sometimes good for someone else (or a policy) to be the "bad guy?"
8. In your opinion, is Dr. Lee likely to leave the conversation with the impression that the principal is supportive of her desire to infuse the Bible curriculum? If so, why?
9. Imagine that the visitor asked the principal directly if she considers herself a Christian and that, if so, she finds it hard to believe that the

principal would not be supportive of the curriculum. In such a case, how should the principal respond?

10. Identify areas in which you believe the principal acted effectively.
11. Identify areas in which you believe the principal could have acted more effectively.

Balcony View

Generally speaking, how did the principal perform in this scenario? What would you have done differently?

Standards In Action

Which standards do you see as relevant in the scenario? Does the principal effectively meet them? Are there standards and/or criteria left unmet by the principal's actions?

Self Check

Picturing yourself in the principal's chair, describe your emotions. Does the case touch any of your biases or prior experiences?

Switch It Up

How might your thinking or approach change if the gender, social class, ethnicity, language, age, sexual orientation or other descriptors of the players involved were different?

Principal's Presence

In televised presidential debates, "looking presidential" is an important measure of a candidate's performance. The same is true for principals. Halpern and Lubar (2003, p. 3) define leadership presence as being more than "commanding attention" to include "the ability to connect authentically with the thoughts and feelings of others." Does the principal exert an effective "Principal's Presence?" Explain.

Principal's Priority

How *serious* is the situation?
How *soon* should the principal address this situation?
Should the principal inform/involve a *supervisor* on this issue?

In A Word

Capture the principal's performance in the scenario using one word.

Collaborate

Collaborate with a classmate or colleague to rewrite or alter the case with a different set of circumstances. Share your new case with other colleagues to ascertain how they would approach it.

Extension & Internship Experiences

- Examine your district policies related to curriculum adoption. What process exists for parents or other stakeholders to propose or question the curriculum? Can members of the administrative team recall recent cases in which the policy was applied?
- Often, particularly in homogeneous communities, educators find themselves under intense pressure to do what is popular, regardless of law or policy. In this case, there may be considerable support for teaching some form of the Bible or Christianity in the curriculum. Research relevant case law and court decisions to determine how a principal can be on solid legal ground. Do you sense community pressure or expectations that school leaders in your community be active members of a particular faith or church?
- Passage of the Equal Access Act (1984) guaranteed that student religious and secular activities have equal access to public school facilities. Since that time, student groups ranging from gay-straight alliances to chess clubs to religious groups have met during non-instructional time. Review the concept of a limited open forum under the Equal Access Act and examine how your school's facilities are used. Interview a building or district level leader about policies controversies related to access to facilities, limited open forums, and non-curricular groups.
- Conduct a search of regional or national news stories involving curricular controversies related to religion in schools. How were the issues resolved? Construct a list of guidelines or a flow chart to guide a principal through the decision making and communication process.

REFERENCES AND RESOURCES

Browder, L. H. (1998). The religious right, the secular left, and their shared dilemma: The public school. *International Journal of Educational Reform, 7*(4), 309–318.
Deckman, M. M. (2004). *School board battles: The Christian Right in local politics.* Washington, D. C.: Georgetown University Press.

Dunklee, D. R., & Shoop, R. J. (2006). *The principal's quick-reference guide to school law: Reducing liability, litigation, and other potential legal tangles.* (2nd ed.). Thousand Oaks, CA: Corwin Press.

Essex, N. L. (2012). *School law and the public schools: A practical guide for educational leaders.* (5th ed.). Upper Saddle River, NJ: Pearson.

Fraser, J. (1999). *Between church and state: Religion and public education in a multicultural America.* New York, NY: St Martin's Griffin.

Greenwalt, K. (2007). *Does God belong in public schools?* Princeton, NJ: Princeton University Press.

La Morte, M. W. (2012). *School law: Cases and concepts.* (10th ed.). Upper Saddle River, NJ: Pearson.

Leahy, M. (1998). The religious right: Would-be censors of the state school curriculum. *Educational Philosophy & Theory, 30*(1), 18, 51.

Lemon v. Kurtzman, 403 U.S. 602 (1971).

Lester, E. (2011). *Teaching about religions: A democratic approach for public schools.* Ann Arbor, MI: University of Michigan Press.

Moore, D. L. (2007). *Overcoming religious illiteracy: A cultural studies approach to the study of religion in secondary education.* New York, NY: Palgrave Macmillan.

Moore, D. L., & the AAR Religion in the Schools Task Force. (2010, April). *Guidelines for teaching about religion in K-12 public schools in the United States.* Atlanta, GA: American Academy of Religion. Retrieved from http://www.aarweb.org/.

Nash, R. J., & Bishop, P. A. (2010). *Teaching adolescents religious literacy in a post 9/11 world.* Charlotte, NC: Information Age Publishing.

Nord, W. A. (2010). *Does God make a difference? Taking religion seriously in our schools and universities.* New York, NY: Oxford University Press.

Nord, W. A., & Haynes, C. C. (1998). *Taking religion seriously across the curriculum.* Alexandria, VA: Association for Supervision and Curriculum Development, 1198.

Stone v. Graham, 599 S.W. 2d 157 (Ky. 1980).

Thomas, R. M. (2007). *God in the classroom: Religion and America's public schools.* Westport, CT: Praeger.

For additional resources, consult the *Religion & Education* journal. The journal's website is: http://www.informaworld.com/urel.

Also, the Society for Biblical Literature offers a number of resources, including *Teaching the Bible*, an e-publication for high school teachers. The publication's website is: http://www.sbl-site.org.

The Josephson Institute Center for Youth Ethics hosts the Character Counts program at: http://www, charactercounts.org.

Appendix

Educational Leadership Constituency Council (ELCC) Standards

ELCC Standard	Element
Standard 1: Candidates who complete the program are educational leaders who have the knowledge and ability to promote the success of all students by facilitating the development, articulation, implementation, and stewardship of a school or district vision of learning supported by the school community.	1.1 Develop a vision 1.2 Articulate a vision 1.3 Implement a vision 1.4 Steward a vision 1.5 Promote community involvement in the vision
Standard 2: Candidates who complete the program are educational leaders who have the knowledge and ability to promote the success of all students by promoting a positive school culture, providing an effective instructional program, applying best practice to student learning, and designing comprehensive professional growth plans for staff.	2.1 Promote positive school culture 2.2 Provide effective instructional program 2.3 Apply best practice to student learning 2.4 Design comprehensive professional growth plan
Standard 3: Candidates who complete the program are educational leaders who have the knowledge and ability to promote the success of all students by managing the organization, operations, and resources in a way that promotes a safe, efficient, and effective learning environment.	3.1 Manage the organization 3.2 Manage operations 3.3 Manage resources

(Continued)

ELCC Standard	*Element*
Standard 4: Candidates who complete the program are educational leaders who have the knowledge and ability to promote the success of all students by collaborating with families and other community members, responding to diverse community interests and needs, and mobilizing community resources.	4.1 Collaborate with families and other community members 4.2 Respond to community interests and needs 4.3 Mobilize community resources
Standard 5: Candidates who complete the program are educational leaders who have the knowledge and ability to promote the success of all students by acting with integrity, fairly, and in an ethical manner.	5.1 Act with integrity 5.2 Act fairly 5.3 Act ethically
Standard 6: Candidates who complete the program are educational leaders who have the knowledge and ability to promote the success of all students by understanding, responding to, and influencing the larger political, social, economic, legal, and cultural context.	6.1 Understand the larger context 6.2 Respond to the larger context 6.3 Influence the larger context

References

Brock, B. L., and Grady, M. L. (2004). *Launching your first principalship: A guide for beginning principals.* Thousand Oaks, CA: Corwin Press.

Darling-Hammond, L., LaPointe, M., Meyerson, D., Orr, M. T., and Cohen, C. (2007). *Preparing school leaders for a changing world: Lessons from exemplary leadership development programs.* Stanford, CA: Stanford University, Stanford Educational Leadership Institute.

Farkas, S., Johnson, J., and Duffett, A. (2003). *Rolling up their sleeves: Superintendents and principals talk about what's needed to fix public schools.* New York, NY: Public Agenda.

Halpern, B. L., and Lubar, K. (2003). *Leadership presence: Dramatic techniques to reach out, motivate, and inspire.* New York, NY: Penguin Group.

Hess, F. M., and Kelly, A. P. (2007). Learning to lead: What gets taught in principal-preparation programs. *Teachers College Record, 109*(1), 244–274.

Kosmoski, G. J., and Pollack, D. R. (2005). *Managing difficult, frustrating, and challenging conversations: Strategies for savvy administrators.* (2nd ed.). Thousand Oaks, CA: Corwin Press.

Levine, A. (2005). *Educating School Leaders.* New York, NY: Teachers College, The Education Schools Project.

McEwan, E. K. (2004). *How to deal with parents who are angry, troubled, afraid, or just plain crazy.* (2nd ed.). Thousand Oaks, CA: Corwin Press.

Murphy, J. T. (2006). Dancing lessons for elephants: Reforming ed school leadership programs. *Phi Delta Kappan, 87*(7), 488–491.

Scott, S. (2004). *Fierce conversations: Achieving success at work & in life, one conversation at a time.* New York, NY: The Berkley Publishing Group.

Southern Regional Education Board (SREB). (2006). *Schools can't wait: Accelerating the redesign of university administration preparation programs.* Retrieved from http://www.wallacefoundation.org

Tooms, A. (2005). *The rookie's playbook: Insights and dirt for new principals.* Lanham, MD: Scarecrow Education.

About the Contributors

Emily Borcherding is a graduate student at the University of Northern Iowa and a graduate assistant for the Educational Leadership department and the UNI Writing Center. After earning her BA in Mathematics and Spanish Teaching from the University of Northern Iowa and three years of high school math teaching and volleyball and basketball coaching, Emily is completing her MA in Postsecondary Education: Student Affairs at UNI. In her spare time she likes to play and watch sports, bike, and listen to and play music.

"PRINCIPALS" AND ACTORS

Dr. Willie Barney is a principal of an urban high school in Waterloo, Iowa. He is working on his superintendency certification through the University of Northern Iowa. Much of Dr. Barney's spare time is spent with his wife Jody and their six children engaging in a wide range of sports and activities. Regardless of what it is that Dr. Barney is doing, he desires to help those that he works with to reach their fullest potential whether it is in school or beyond.

Amber N. Boyd serves as an administrator at West High School in Waterloo, Iowa. She holds a BA from Wartburg College in American and World history, an MA in Curriculum and Instruction from the University of Northern Iowa, an MA in Effective Teaching: Talented and Gifted from Drake University and is also nearing completion of a doctorate in Educational Leadership from UNI. Amber runs a program at the high school level called Girls to Women that focuses on self-efficacy and self-empowerment in African American young ladies. She enjoys spending time with friends and family and working in her church. Amber plans to pursue a principalship in the Waterloo Community School district.

Todd Coulter is finishing his seventh year as school administrator in the Waterloo Community School District in Waterloo, Iowa. He currently serves as the Athletic Director at his alma mater, Waterloo East High School. Prior to entering administration Todd taught physical education and health at all levels. When not at school or supervising athletic events, Todd likes to watch his three children in their various sports activities and also run in 5K road races in the summertime.

Dan Cox serves as Principal at Hoover Middle School in Waterloo, Iowa. He holds a BA in Social Science, an MA in Spanish, and his principalship endorsement, all from the University of Northern Iowa. He received his superintendency endorsement from Iowa State University where he is finishing his Ph.D. in Educational Leadership. A former high school Spanish teacher and coach, Dan has lived abroad (Spain & Argentina) and enjoys traveling the world. He currently resides in Hudson, Iowa.

Jon Cox coordinates the Minority Student & Diversity Program for the University of Northern Iowa's College of Business Administration. A former college basketball player and coach, Jon has also served as a chief of school security. He lives with his wife and son in Waterloo, Iowa, where he is active in youth mentoring programs.

Jeff Dieken has been a high school principal for four years in the Hudson Community School District in Hudson, Iowa. Prior to receiving his MA in the principalship from the University of Northern Iowa, Jeff taught high school English at Waterloo (IA) West High School. An avid sports fan, Jeff, his wife (also in education), and two daughters attend most Northern Iowa football and basketball games. Jeff plans to continue his studies in Educational Leadership.

Deb Donlea is a fourth grade teacher at Center Point-Urbana Elementary School in Center Point, Iowa. She is nearing completion of her MA in the principalship from the University of Northern Iowa and plans to pursue an elementary school principalship. Deb, an avid cyclist, lives in Winthrop, Iowa with her husband, Jason, and two daughters.

Anel Garza Sandoval is a second grade bilingual teacher at Woodbury Elementary in Marshalltown, Iowa. She is nearing completion of her MA in the principalship from the University of Northern Iowa and plans to pursue an elementary principalship at a bilingual school. Anel lives in Marshalltown, Iowa with her husband, Jose, and their two children.

Kyle Green is the Head Men's Basketball Coach at the University of Wisconsin-Eau Claire. He has been a college basketball coach at the Division I, II and III levels for the past 17 years and also spent three years as a junior high and high school social studies teacher in Minneapolis, Minnesota. Kyle played collegiate basketball at Hamline University in St. Paul, Minnesota, graduating in 1992. Following his collegiate playing career, he spent one year playing professionally in Denmark. Kyle is married and the father of an 11 year old boy and a 9 year old girl.

Amy Hawkins serves as the District Athletic Coordinator and Wellness Curriculum Director for the Dubuque Community School District in Dubuque, Iowa. She holds a Bachelor's degree in education from Winona State University and an MA in the principalship from the University of Northern Iowa. A former college volleyball player, Amy has also coached at the high school and college levels. Amy and her husband Jeremy live in Dubuque, Iowa with their two daughters Madelyn and Morgan.

Gwen Hefel-Busch is currently a valued member of Thomas Jefferson Middle School in Dubuque, Iowa and serves as the department chair for special education. She started her career by earning her Bachelor's degree from the University of Dubuque in 1998 and completed her MA in the principalship from the University of Northern Iowa in 2010. Her background involves teaching in a self-contained behavior disorder classroom at the middle school level for ten years. Through her dedication and commitment to her students, she earned Wal-Mart's Dubuque Teacher of the Year award in 2005. Now as department chair, she serves as a liaison between classroom teachers, Area Education Agency consultants, and administration. Gwen has also become a certified Crisis Intervention Prevention trainer who works with district staff in the art of classroom management and de-escalation techniques. Another important aspect of her position is to serve as the Medicaid lead teacher. Gwen enjoys spending quality time with her husband and three children.

Roark Horn is currently the Chief Administrator for Area Education Agency 267, an educational service provider helping 60 school districts in North Central Iowa. He earned his Ed.D. at the University of Northern Iowa and also completed all of his administrative certifications at that institution. Roark's past work has included two superintendent positions, a high school principalship, and a service as a classroom teacher. He and his wife Jean have three children and live in Hudson, Iowa.

Jeremy Jones is Dean of Students at South Tama County Middle School in Toledo, IA. He is completing his MA in the principalship from the University of Northern Iowa. He lives with his wife, Michelle, and two-year old twins, Blake and Alexandra.

Jeremy Langner is an Assistant Principal at Waterloo West High School in Waterloo, Iowa, which serves approximately 1600 students. He earned his undergraduate and MA in the principalship at the University of Northern Iowa. Jeremy's past work has included teaching social studies an service as an administrative assistant, and a high school baseball, basketball and football coach. Jeremy and his wife Becky, a second grade teacher, have one child and live in Denver, Iowa.

Debbie Lee is the Director of Secondary Curriculum for the Waterloo Community Schools (WCSD) in Waterloo, Iowa. She has had over 30 years of experience as a teacher and administrator in general education and special education, including 15 years of teaching internationally in Germany, Japan, and India. She earned her doctorate at the University of Northern Iowa in curriculum and instruction and has a passion for collaborating with principals, teachers, and instructional coaches to advance student achievement. Her current work includes guiding initiatives in curriculum and instruction, organizing and providing professional development, guiding instructional coaches, and participating in various committees, including the UNI/WCSD Professional Development Schools project. She is the mother of two adult sons, enjoys the company of a delightful granddaughter, and is married to a middle school instructional math coach. She loves to read, travel, entertain, and laugh.

Jane Lindaman serves as Associate Superintendent for Educational Services in the Waterloo Community School District in Waterloo, Iowa. She holds a Bachelor's degree in middle school education and MA and doctorate degrees in educational leadership from University of Northern Iowa. She served as a middle school principal for 12 years and has been in central office administration for the past five years. Jane and her husband, Steve, live in Cedar Falls, Iowa, with their two young sons.

Heather McDonald is a language arts teacher at Denver Schools in Denver, Iowa. She holds a MA in English from the University of Northern Iowa. After completing a MA in the principalship in 2011, she plans to pursue a secondary principal position. Heather enjoys traveling and reading. She lives with her husband in Waterloo, Iowa.

Tesha Moser serves as principal at Bernard Elementary and Cascade Elementary in the Western Dubuque (IA) County Community School District. She grew up in Elkader, Iowa and then completed her undergraduate degree in education with reading and language arts endorsements at Mount Mercy College in Cedar Rapids, Iowa. Tesha taught first grade at Edgewood-Colesburg Community School District for three years before moving to the Linn-Mar Community School District to teach second grade for a year. She then took a School Administration Manager (SAM) position for two years at Bowman Woods Elementary and loved every minute of administration. Tesha graduated from the University of Northern Iowa in May of 2010 with her MA in the principalship and began her current position. In her free time Tesha enjoys the outdoors by fishing, golfing, boating, and running. She also enjoys spending time with her family, friends, and fiancé Jeff.

Emily O' Donnell teaches math at North Central Junior High in North Liberty, Iowa. She also serves as an Elementary Math Curriculum Specialist for the Iowa City Community School District. She holds a Bachelor's degree in Mathematics Education from the University of Iowa, an MA in Middle School Mathematics from the University of Northern Iowa (UNI) and is nearing the completion of her Advanced Studies Certificate (ASC) in the principalship. Emily lives in North Liberty, Iowa, with her husband and three sons. Emily enjoys athletics and being outdoors.

Angela Olsen is an 8th grade math teacher at Spirit Lake Middle School in Spirit Lake, Iowa, teaching 8th grade math and 8th grade algebra. Her experiences range from 11 years teaching high school math in Algona, Iowa and Estherville, Iowa to the last four at the middle school level in Spirit Lake. Angela is pursuing an MA in the principalship through the University of Northern Iowa and will graduate in December of 2011. Angela, her husband, Shawn, and two children, Kyler and Karli, live in Spirit Lake. She enjoys spending time with her family, outdoor activities, and working out.

Heather Olsen, Ed.D. is an assistant professor in the Leisure, Youth, and Human Service Division in the College of Education at the University of Northern Iowa. She is also the Associate Director for the National Program for Playground Safety (NPPS). She has been associated with the development of children's outdoor play areas and educating the public about maintenance, supervision, and age appropriateness, given presentations throughout the country about the design of safe playgrounds and has written many articles on creating playgrounds for children. She directs and teaches the online training programs for NPPS. Dr. Olsen's research interests include outdoor play and learning environments for children and learning styles for adult learners.

Dameon Place is the high school band director in Winterset, Iowa. He is currently finishing his MA work in the principalship from the University of Northern Iowa. Dameon plans to pursue an elementary school principalship.

Dameon enjoys spending time outdoors camping and canoeing as well as home renovation projects. His wife, Lindsay, is a preschool teacher turned stay at home mom with their first son Henry—a future tuba star!

Dan Scannell serves as the special education department chair at Waterloo West High School in Waterloo, Iowa. He earned his MA in the principalship from the University of Northern Iowa and plans to pursue the next step in his career as a principal. In his leisure time, Dan enjoys live music, mountains, and Notre Dame Football. Dan lives in Waterloo, Iowa with his wife, Heather, and his daughter, Ann Grace.

Troy Smock teaches physical education at Center Point-Urbana High School in Center Point, Iowa. He is nearing completion of his MA in education degree from the University of Northern Iowa. He has coached a number of different sports and is the student booster club advisor. Troy's wife teaches 3rd grade at Center Point-Urbana and they have 2 children.

Marybeth C. Stalp is an Associate Professor of Sociology at the University of Northern Iowa. She received her BA in Sociology, Communications and English Literature from Regis University, her MA in Sociology from Southern Illinois University at Carbondale, a graduate certificate in Women's Studies and a Ph.D. in Sociology, both from the University of Georgia. Her research is centered in gender, leisure, and culture in the U.S., and includes women quilters, the Red Hat Society and artists. Her recent work includes the book, "Quilting: The Fabric of Everyday Life" and research articles appearing in the Journal of Contemporary Ethnography, Journal of Leisure Research, Sociological Perspectives, Journal of Women & Aging, Sociological Focus, and Textile: The Journal of Cloth & Culture. Marybeth currently serves as Co-Editor of the Journal of Contemporary Ethnography.

David W. Stamp is a trial lawyer practicing in Waterloo, Iowa. He received his bachelor's degree from the University of Northern Iowa and his law degree from the University of Iowa College of Law. David, his wife Linda, and all three of their sons are active in music and theater. David enjoys any opportunity to be on a stage, whether it is public speaking at a professional seminar, acting in a community theater play, or performing in a local bar band. However, all of his sons are more talented than he is at all of these things, so you should see them when you can.

Matthew P. Tullis serves as the Director of Equity and Learning Supports for the Marshalltown Community School District in Marshalltown, Iowa. He holds a Bachelor's degree in elementary education from the University of Northern Iowa and an MA in education from Viterbo University. He is nearing the completion of an Advanced Studies Certificate in the PK-12

Principalship. He is involved in many community organizations in his hometown of Marshalltown and is an avid runner, cyclist, and swimmer. Matthew and his wife Christine have two children, Austin and Brooke.

Karen Weires is a high school mathematics teacher in Dubuque, Iowa who holds an MA in the teaching of mathematics from the University of Illinois at Chicago. She will soon be completing the Principalship Program at the University of Northern Iowa.

VIDEO PRODUCTION

Paige Besler is a junior at the University of Northern Iowa majoring in General Communication, with minors in Leisure, Youth, and Human Services and Graphic Technologies. Paige is the goalie and co-captain of the UNI Women's Club Soccer team. She is also a member of the UNI chapter for Habitat for Humanity. Paige likes to play different intramural sports every year and play in a slow pitch softball league during the summer. She has worked for Joe Marchesani as an AV Production Assistant for three years.

Gregory LaVern Lilly was born and raised in the dairy hills of the southwestern tip of Iowa. He is currently a junior at the University of Northern Iowa where he is juggling two majors in Business Marketing and Electronic Media with an emphasis in advertising. He is Vice President of Cedar River Productions and holds two on-campus jobs. In Greg's limited free time, he enjoys kayaking, rock climbing, and traveling, and he makes a mean home-made brisket.

Joe Marchesani is currently the Audio/Video Production Coordinator for ITS-Educational Technology and also an Assistant Professor of Education in the Department of Curriculum and Instruction at the University of Northern Iowa, where he has been since 1972. Joe received a BA in Communications from Fordham University and an MS in Speech with a Television Production Emphasis from Brooklyn College, both in New York City. He also obtained a MEd in Educational Media from Temple University in Philadelphia. His wife (Joan), son (David), and daughter (Kristina) all received degrees from UNI, and his son and daughter also work there.